BECOMING INVALUABLE

Develop the Willtitude to Navigotiate Success

Steven Bowen & Terry Lyles, Ph.D.

Becoming Invaluable

Published by MindStir Media, LLC
45 Lafayette Rd | Suite 181| North Hampton, NH 03862 | USA
1.800.767.0531 | www.mindstirmedia.com
Printed in the United States of America.

ISBN-13: 978-1-961532-80-9

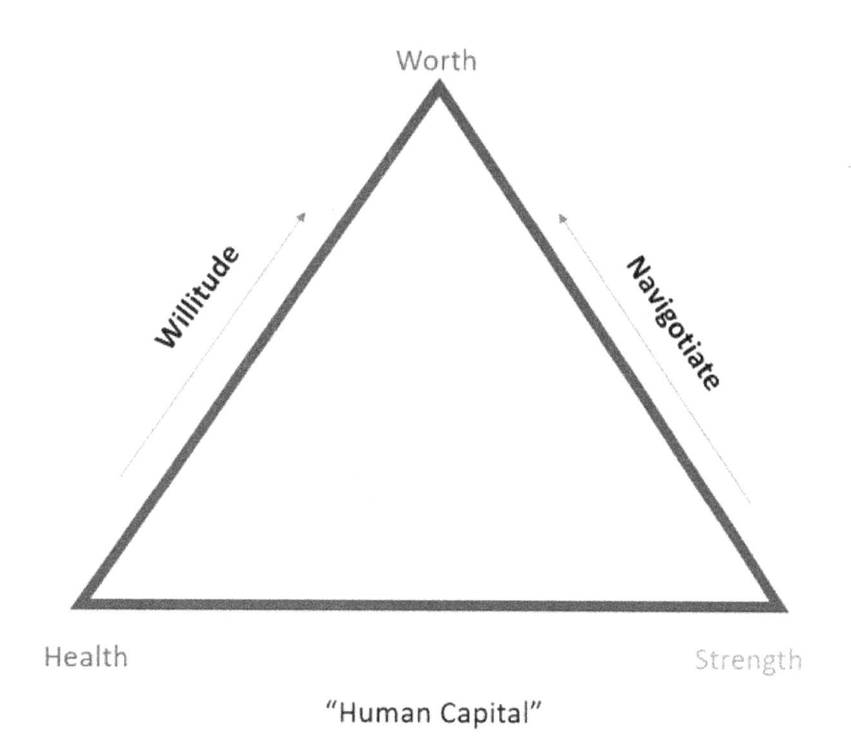

Becoming Invaluable

CONTENTS

PREFACE

While in the process of writing our book, we both discovered some unique insights from our personal lives. We'd like to share them with you here.

Terry

Growing up in the inner city of Indianapolis made me feel the limitations of the dreams and aspirations that should normally lead to outstanding life accomplishments, but my mind and passion to experience the world outside my hood always burned within my soul. I just needed some faith, direction, and created luck! Transitions come and go, but life is all about having navigational awareness and the ability to make course corrections as you pursue your goal. Only then can you accomplish the deepest desires and dreams you could ever imagine. My dream was, and still is, to impact the world with hope and change for a more complete life experience with everyone I meet. This process is not without bumps in the road, but making those bumps more level is the transition between human potential and an unfolding life success story.

I have traveled the world and lived in six states, but one thing is certain: I was always moving toward a life filled with faith and certainty of a better life experience. From marriage to children to work fulfillment beyond my wildest imagination, with a plan to navigotiate and the willitude to succeed, nothing is impossible to those who believe in the possible. This is my story, and I'm sticking to it to encourage you to never, ever give up or give in to mediocracy. Special thanks to my lovely wife Marsha and son Brayden who are always in my corner cheering me on to never stop moving forward toward becoming invaluable. To my son Brandon, who recently passed to the invaluable place of Heaven. His voice, though he never spoke a word in his entire life, still impacts my thoughts and emotions every day. His inspiration in my life will continue to drive me even throughout the writing of this book. Brandon, thank you for being the wind beneath my wings, and I look forward to seeing you again when I'm finished down here! Live out loud today with meaning and purpose, making life whole and satisfying with your dreams and aspirations right in front of you. Become invaluable, and enjoy this book's step-by-step process on how that can become your reality too!

Steve

Looking back, I recall so many lessons in life and numerous goals and values I've carried forward as a result. From my perspective, one of the most important lessons in life is to live with established values, as they are your guidepost to how you treat yourself and others. Goals are also key, because if you have no set direction, life will take you for a ride versus you driving yourself through it. Goals, they change, advance, and become more challenging as life grows.

My mother always told my sister and me that if we wanted to amount to something in life, we needed to go beyond our hometown of Washington, Missouri and experience the world. We did, each following our own pathways. I watched our father, with a high school GED from the military, go from driving a Dr. Pepper/7up delivery truck to having a successful career in manufacturing management. He involved himself in several entrepreneurial ventures with some success, making enough money to be comfortable but not truly wealthy. I can remember watching those experiences and thinking that was not going to be me. I was going to become wealthy, even though I had no idea how.

When I was twenty-five, I set a goal that by age fifty I would have a net worth of eight figures. Goals have a way of advancing and growing over the years, and after I built a successful company I have been blessed to achieve a level of wealth far beyond my original goal. You can too, whatever the goal or focus is in your life. I found in the journey that there are not just one or two key transitional moments that produce these results. In life, there are numerous transitions, and the most significant of them you carry forward with you throughout the years.

The transitions began in earnest early in life, in fourth grade as a result of Mrs. Risch, who presented me with the lesson that to lie is never a winning way. A few years later, I made a change by my own choice for reasons of not allowing others to define me and a desire to learn. I moved from the Catholic school to the public high school in my hometown, something that did not go down well at first with my very devoutly Catholic mother, but she still supported my desire for change. The next transition, there was a wakeup call from my father about my grades in college, which he delivered at Christmas time during my sophomore year. I heeded the call and graduated with the top honors of those receiving a BA in chemistry along with having been very involved in student government. Then came the transition to the work world, followed by the unexpected change after a flight, less than a year out of college, and made a move from my first to second job in sales.

This transition facilitated more than just early career success. It led to a key to my life's success by meeting Deb, my future wife of thirty-eight years, having our children, Grant and Natalie, followed by my biggest career move from sales into consulting. When this transition to consulting occurred, little did I know at the time that Larry Williams provided me with the learning opportunity of my career, forming my foundation in sales and marketing that I would utilize to excel throughout life.

As Terry and I write this book, I find myself in transition again. After building and selling a successful consulting company, I am now transitioning into the so-called retirement phase of life. I have realized I love transitions in life. You learn a great deal and can expand yourself in so many ways, if you are equipped with the tools to transform yourself. These include the willitude to succeed and the ability to navigotiate the challenges you encounter throughout the journey of life, as well as the knowledge, skills, and attitude to drive improvements and changes first and foremost within yourself. More ahead on these new words: willitude and navigotiate.

I thank my mother and father, Mrs. Risch, Bob Wunderlich, (who was the first person I admired as a successful businessperson and was a close friend of my father), Larry Williams, and several others who helped shape my life. Most of all, I thank my wife Deb for all the years of support and letting me share with her and gain her perspective regarding various business situations, for raising our two beautiful and successful children, and of course for putting up with me and how I've been in life for the past four decades and what I hope and plan to be the rest of my life. Thank you, Deb, and each of you are a true blessing in my life. Again, thank you all!

I have read nearly two hundred books, listened to thousands of recordings on self-development, and enjoyed every moment of the learning. I hope everyone in their life's journey, whatever career or vocation you have chosen, can be prepared, learn, and experience the outcomes you design for yourself. This is my desire in co-authoring this book with Terry, to provide a few perspectives and tools that make a real difference.

INTRODUCTION

This book started with a basic idea of Becoming Invaluable as a person, team, or company.

In-Val-U-Able as you will learn means health, strength and worth in becoming a better you! Everyone is capable of becoming invaluable, the knowledge and skill needed to accomplish invaluableness has to often be revealed to us. We have discovered over years from our own learning through the actual application of the techniques in this book from growing companies, to winning races, making money, staying healthy, and assisting performers in becoming the best of the best.

We have a simple question to ask. Here it is:

"What do you think is the highest calling in life you can have?"

One answer could be to become a successful CEO of a big, influential company.

That's a good response.

Or you may aspire to be an esteemed doctor and save countless lives.

That would be admirable.

How about a famous actor or musician who entertains millions of people?

Not bad at all!

One more choice ... What if you made the life of just one other person brighter and more beautiful?

Wait—really? Just one other person?

Yes. If you believe that human life is priceless, then wouldn't impacting one other person be meaningful? That person could be a child, a sick neighbor, or someone facing difficult circumstances.

Yes, that would be a high calling in life.

Assuming your intent is positive, all of these choices and many more have one thing in common.

This one commonality is that you have made yourself *invaluable* to the people or person you serve. You provide a service or support that no one else could. Without you and your direct involvement, the people you serve would not be the same. They would be relatively impoverished—physically, emotionally, spiritually. Because you are invaluable to them, their lives are better, and they can reach their human potential.

To become invaluable to a person, a family, a community, or even a nation is one of the most satisfying things you can do in life. It's true that you do it for yourself, but you cannot do it without serving other people and making their lives better. In that regard, it's a win-win situation. You win because they win.

But there's one catch.

Being invaluable and making a positive difference to one person or an entire community requires certain personal attributes. Unless you have these attributes, you may not be able to make your goal a reality. You may have the best of intentions, but good intentions must be translated into *action*. Being invaluable takes *work*. It may be pleasant and rewarding work, but the effort must be expended, usually every day.

To do the work and become invaluable requires five personal attributes. They are knowledge, skills, attitude, health, and strength.

This book will show you how to develop those five key personal attributes so that you can become invaluable. The development of those attributes takes commitment and effort, but the good news is the payback: You'll feel better and better every day. Your sense of self-worth and well-being will increase. You'll be more engaged with life and derive more enjoyment from everything you do.

In addition to the five key personal attributes, to become truly invaluable you'll also need four others: a set of values to guide you in the right direction, a purpose in life, a sense of willitude, and the ability to navigotiate.

You may not recognize those last two words—willitude and navigotiate. That's okay, because they're new words created just for this book. Basically, willitude is a combination of willpower and fortitude. And navigotiate is a combination of navigate and negotiate. We've put them together to form new words that relate directly to your ability to become invaluable.

Throughout the book, you'll find plenty of inspiring real-life stories (as well as a few cautionary tales!), including some from our own lives. In addition, the Invaluable Spotlight Profiles you will find laced throughout are from many different individuals and perspectives. These stories of our interviewees are from their real-life experiences including both failures and successes, and they have one thing in common. They trace the individual's personal journey to becoming invaluable in the way that fit their personal goals. Perhaps in a future edition of *Becoming Invaluable* we'll be able to include your story as well!

In addition, after each chapter you'll find a set of Action Steps, called the Bottom Line. These are handy reminders of the highlights of the chapter and the positive actions you can take to support your journey to becoming invaluable.

Our desire for this book is to inspire, motivate, educate, and support you in whatever your walk of life. Regardless of your vocation, career, or path in life, you can enhance your outcomes and the experiences along the way through the application of the methods you will find throughout this book. You can find through our website and social media pages a variety of tools and ways to enhance your learning and journey. This book is available as an Audio Book, in Spanish as well as podcasts and social media posts. Visit us at www.becominginvaluable.com Ready? Let's get started!

FIND YOUR VALUE

From a moral standpoint, every human life has equivalent value. Whether you are a king or a peasant, rich or poor, boss or worker, your life is just as precious as anyone else's. When you vote in an election, your vote counts the same as any other person's, regardless of their station in life. In fact, this rule was enshrined in our Declaration of Independence by Thomas Jefferson, who wrote, "We hold these truths to be self-evident, that all men are created equal, that they are endowed by their Creator with certain unalienable Rights, that among these are Life, Liberty and the pursuit of Happiness." These days we substitute "people" for "men," but you get the idea. We want no king lording over us. We want everyone to have an equal opportunity to succeed. Simply said, *value* is the importance of something or someone that defines significance in life. Everything has some quantity of value, but the beauty or worth is measured by the opinion of the one who wants that valued possession.

That's the way it is in law and ethical philosophy. But let's look at the question more narrowly. Ever since early humans decided to walk upright, the hard truth is that each one of us must *work* to support ourselves. By "work," we mean perform some task that brings a material compensation to ourselves, our family, and our community. That task could be just about anything—hunting, farming, manufacturing, having children, making art, defending the tribe against attackers. The list of occupations or vocations that bring *value* to the individual and the group is long, as we will reference in the pages ahead. The good news is that our work need not be drudgery; to the contrary, many people who toil very hard would describe their vocation as enjoyable. The most successful people will tell you they *love* their work. Have you ever heard Paul McCartney, Oprah Winfrey, Tom Brady, or Warren Buffett say they dislike their jobs? Hardly!

But here's another honest fact. While every human is intrinsically of equal worth—that is, priceless—not every *occupation* is of equal economic value. In fact, how people choose to spend their time results in tremendous differences in value as measured by the money they're paid or the level of recognition they receive. Some jobs are low-paying and commonplace, while others are considered extremely valuable.

For example, consider the fast-food giant McDonald's. The entry level wage for kitchen help at a typical McDonald's restaurant is about $15.00 per hour. If you worked thirty-five hours a week with no vacation, that would be about $27,300 per year. If you have that job, that's your current value in the job market. You may be a nice person and even well educated, but if you're working the fryolator, that's your current market value.

At the other end of the scale, consider the CEO of McDonald's—the person at the top of the fast-food empire's totem pole. In 2021, Chris Kempczinski received a total pay package of just over $20 million. That means that if he worked the same thirty-five-hour week as the fryolator guy, his hourly value would have been nearly $11,000 per hour. Chris Kempczinski could work *two and a half hours* to make what the fryolator guy made *in an entire year.*

Is the fryolator guy *valuable* to McDonald's? Only slightly. He could be easily replaced. His work has some value, especially to his co-workers, but not very much.

On the other hand, is the CEO *irreplaceable?* If he quit or decided to retire to Bali, could he be replaced by another top executive? Yes, of course. Leaders are replaced all the time.

Very few people are truly irreplaceable. Most of them are artists of some type. There is no replacement for Mick Jagger, J.K. Rowling, or Steven Spielberg. When they're gone, the void will be permanent. There's no doubt these artists love their vocations and generate great happiness as they live out their occupations.

This book is about being *invaluable.* It means being as close to irreplaceable as you can get. It means having the knowledge, skill, experience, talent, or productivity that others cannot match. When you're invaluable, it means that you have a special ability or competence that others don't have, for which the market will pay a premium or provide high levels of emotionally positive feedback.

Ways to Become Invaluable

In our society, we measure our value by many different yardsticks. Some are easy to identify while others are more nuanced. Here are some of the paths you take to become invaluable to your family, business, or community.

Invent, Make, or Sell Something Valuable

One of the most obvious ways to become invaluable is to invent, make, or sell a physical object that has utility people want. Your products might include computers, cars, electronic devices, clothing, houses, or solar panels. It might be food, such as coffee. People who have become household names by doing this include Steve Jobs, Henry Ford, Elon Musk, Sir Richard Branson, Howard Schultz, and Bill Gates. But it also depends on the size of your community. If you live in a small town in the middle of farm country and own the local hardware store, you might be invaluable to the farmers who live in the area.

Provide a Valuable Service

You could be a doctor, lawyer, business consultant, or personal advisor. In this case, you're selling or offering your specialized subject matter knowledge to people who need it. Knowledge of difficult subjects has real value, and the more difficult the subject with high value attached to it, the more invaluable you're going to be. For example, if you can solve a Rubik's cube in less than 3.47 seconds (the current record), you'll be famous among people who follow the sport of Rubik's cube solving, but the subject doesn't have a high value attached to it. But if you could solve the riddle of Alzheimer's disease and provide the cure, you'd be hailed around the world and take your rightful place among humanity's greatest heroes. And if you're a family doctor or primary caregiver and you save your patient from succumbing to a terrible disease, then you'll be invaluable to them.

Civic or Business Leadership

You can enter politics and provide inspiring leadership on the local, state, or federal level. We remember all US presidents, but some, such as George Washington and Abraham Lincoln, are seen by most people as being truly invaluable to their nation.

Within organizations and businesses, effective leaders are invaluable. People like Tim Cook at Apple, Sheryl Sandburg at Facebook, Bob Iger at Disney, and Mary Barra at General Motors regularly appear on lists of the most influential or respected business leaders.

This brings us to a point worth mentioning: To be invaluable within your community does not necessarily mean you are universally loved by every human being on earth! Humans hold a wide variety of viewpoints and opinions, and a leader who is respected and admired by one group may be dismissed or even reviled by another. The politician who's seen by his or her party as a hero and champion will be criticized and opposed by members of the other party. (What you can hope for, and should strive for, is to be *respected* by your political opponents, even if they disagree with you!)

Again, the scale of the stage on which you operate makes a difference. Many people in small towns are happy to serve their community and become invaluable to it without aspiring to higher office. That's fine as long as you're rising to the level you know is right for you. No one can determine that but you.

Moral or Spiritual Leadership

Outside of your immediate family, an invaluable adult may have been a pastor, a Scout leader, or a coach.

We celebrate national leaders who never held elective office but were invaluable to the development of the nation, such as Dr. Martin Luther King, Jr., or globally, such as Gandhi or Nelson Mandela (who did get elected president of South Africa after being released from prison in 1990). We look up to religious and spiritual leaders including the Dalai Lama, Deepak Chopra, the Pope, Ravi Shanker, and others. Many such people have little wealth or worldly power, and their influence comes from their quiet persuasion and wise words dispensed over many years.

Science

Many people become invaluable when they expand the bounds of human knowledge, which leads to new technologies and solutions to human problems. We celebrate great thinkers from ancient times, such as Plato and Confucius, and all the luminaries throughout history from Isaac Newton to Albert Einstein. These philosophers and scientists didn't produce products to sell or provide a service; they provided others with the tools and knowledge to make human life better.

Many such gifted people labor in relative obscurity only to be hailed later in life. A good example is the trio of Black women "computers" who in the early 1960s played a vital role in advancing American space travel. Using only slide rules and adding machines, Mary Jackson, Katherine Johnson, and Dorothy Vaughan provided NASA with precise and accurate computations for rocketry and space travel. In fact, John Glenn, the first American to orbit the earth in 1962, would not agree to board the rocket until the three women had approved the flight calculations. Their invaluable achievements were largely unknown until the release of the movie *Hidden Figures*, based on the book of the same name by Margot Lee Shetterly. It just goes to show you that sometimes the most invaluable people are the ones laboring behind the scenes, out of the public eye.

Military or Police Leadership

We live in a civil society where we have laws that we mutually agree to obey, and likewise our nation shares the globe with many other nations. In our country, citizens are not required to take the law into their own hands, as they may have done on the wild frontier a hundred years ago. In fact, citizens are forbidden from doing that. That's why we have professional police forces and a professional national military. Every individual law enforcement officer is invaluable, as is every soldier, sailor, or airman. And within military and law enforcement organizations, there's a clear hierarchy. In the US military, for example, you might say the most invaluable person is the chairman of the Joint Chiefs of Staff.

Most soldiers and police officers have successful but uneventful careers, but you never know when events will compel a public servant to step up and become invaluable. Such a moment occurred on March 24, 2023, when an armed shooter entered The Covenant School in Nashville and opened fire. Among the initial five Metro Nashville Police on the scene were officers Rex Engelbert, a four-year veteran, and Michael Collazo, a nine-year veteran. Without hesitation, they entered the school, searched for and found the heavily armed attacker, and quickly ended her life. Sadly, six students and teachers had already been killed, but officials agreed that the heroism of officers Engelbert and Collazo had prevented many more deaths. With little thought of their own safety, they ran straight into danger and by their actions earned the external respect and esteem of not just the school and the city but the entire nation. And what they did has had the effect of making every police officer and first responder ask themselves, "What would I do if I were in that situation someday? Would I run into the school, the burning building, or anywhere where people were in immediate danger?" You never know until it happens to you.

Teacher

If making a lot of money is not a requirement for you, then who would argue that some of the most invaluable people in the world are those who teach our children?

Teachers contribute to our children's social, intellectual, and psychological development. They help shape the minds of future generations and encourage students to become their best selves and pursue their own dreams of becoming invaluable members of society. They have the opportunity to interact with students at all stages of development and from all walks of life and are in a position where they can instill values in their students. A great teacher wants to help students along life's path and play a part in shaping the person they will ultimately become.

During the school day, teachers never stop their whirlwind of roles as surrogate mother or father, counselor, police officer, role model, and mentor. They come to school early, stay late, and work nights and weekends to prepare their lesson plans. They tutor students, grade papers, put lesson plans online, meet with parents, call and email administrators and counselors—the list is endless.

They may even be called upon to defend their students. In the section above, we highlighted two invaluable police officers at The Covenant School. One of the six victims that day was

Katherine Koonce, head of The Covenant School. When the shooter started firing, Koonce was on a Zoom call. She immediately ended the call and went out into the hallway, where evidence suggests she confronted the intruder before being shot.

Koonce was described by friends as a smart and loving female leader within a generally male-led religious culture. "If there was any trouble in that school, she would run to it, not from it," Jackie Bailey, a family friend, said of Koonce. "She was trying to protect those kids... That's just what I believe."

"She gave her life to protect the students she loved," Koonce's family said in a statement to the local newspaper, *The Tennessean*.[1]

As you think back to your school days, you can probably name a teacher who had a profound impact on you. This teacher was probably neither famous nor highly paid, and yet he or she was invaluable to you and to many other students. Teachers tend to be remembered because their interactions with their students are regular and structured toward a goal. But when you're a teacher, you never know which of the hundreds of seeds you plant will grow into a mighty tree!

Steve Jobs credited his fourth grade teacher, Imogene "Teddy" Hill, with transforming him from a rebellious misfit into a real student: "She taught an advanced fourth grade class, and it took her about a month to get hip to my situation. She bribed me into learning. She would say, 'I really want you to finish this workbook. I'll give you five bucks if you finish it.' That really kindled a passion in me for learning things! I learned more that year than I think I learned in any other year in school."[2]

---

1 https://www.tennessean.com/story/news/local/2023/03/30/nashville-shooting-victim-katherine-koonce-died-protecting-students/70054488007/

2 Isaacson, Walter (2011). Steve Jobs (1st ed.). New York, NY: Simon & Schuster. ISBN 978-1-4516-4853-9.

The renowned writer and poet Maya Angelou has credited her teacher, Mrs. Flower, who would take her to the library and encourage her to read all the books and read the poetry aloud along with her, which opened Angelou's mind and heart to the power of words.

Likewise for Oprah Winfrey, who has praised her teacher, Mrs. Duncan: "I always, because of Mrs. Duncan, felt I could take on the world. She did exactly what teachers are supposed to do, they create a spark for learning that lives with you from then on. It's why I have a talk show today."[3]

Here's one more word of praise for a teacher, from Bill Nye, The Science Guy: "It was Mr. Lang, my teacher, who loved physics, who got me excited about airplanes, mechanisms, and electronics."[4]

Who could know that Mr. Lang's efforts to encourage young Bill Nye to develop his interest in science would have the result it did?

Arts and Entertainment

There are many artists, writers, musicians, filmmakers, and others creative people without whom our everyday lives would be very different.

Imagine—to borrow a word from John Lennon—life without The Beatles, Mozart or Beethoven. How about the great artists like Picasso and Vincent van Gogh? Or filmmakers such as Steven Spielberg and performers including Marilyn Monroe or Harrison Ford? How about writers like Shakespeare and JK Rowling? These and so many others define our culture and our lives and are truly invaluable. Sometimes their value grows

---

3 https://scoonews.com/news/news-10-celeb-quotes-thanking-their-favourite-school-teachers-for-success-9045/

4 https://wardsworld.wardsci.com/stem-makerspace/world-teacher-s-day-9-famously-successful-people-who-gave-thanks-to-teachers

only after they're gone, as in the case of van Gogh, who sold only one or two of his paintings in his lifetime. His stature slowly grew, and in 1990—the last time a major work by the artist was sold—his *Portrait of Dr. Paul Gachet*—went for a record $83 million. His works are at the core of any art history education, and his influence has been immense.

Be Invaluable to One Person

At first, this may seem absurd. Be invaluable to just one person?

Yes. A child or a friend in need. Even perhaps a stranger. You never know the effect you might have on that person and what they may go on to accomplish in life.

The one person to whom you are invaluable could be your own child. There are countless successful people who credit their parents—or single mom or dad—with lighting the fire in their hearts and spurring them on to big things.

You can adopt an orphaned child and be forever invaluable to them.

You can visit a sick person in the hospital, and they'll never forget your kindness.

You can be invaluable to your own parents as they get older and need personal care.

Many successful—even invaluable—people have publicly thanked their mother, father, or other caregiver. For example, the great Muhammad Ali said this about his parents, Cassius Marcellus Clay Sr., a sign and billboard painter, and his mother, Odessa O'Grady Clay, a household domestic: "My mother once told me that my confidence in myself made her believe in me. I thought that was funny, because it was her confidence in me that strengthened my belief in myself. I didn't realize it then, but from the very beginning, my parents were helping me build the foundation for my life."[5]

Here's another example. These days, Taylor Swift is arguably the most successful pop music performer on the planet. To her millions of fans, she's invaluable! Her parents, Scott Kingsley Swift and Andrea Gardner Swift, supported her dreams of becoming a professional singer, and when Taylor was just eleven years old her mother began driving her from their home in Wyomissing, Pennsylvania to knock on doors of record companies in Nashville. When Taylor was fourteen, to boost her career the family moved from Wyomissing to Hendersonville, Tennessee, and her father, a stockbroker, transferred to the Nashville office of Merrill Lynch. At age seventeen, Taylor released her first album, *Taylor Swift*—and the rest is history. In 2011, Taylor showed her appreciation for her parents by buying them an historic mansion worth $2.5 million in Nashville. Known as the "Northumberland Estate," it was built in 1925 and includes hundreds of acres of rolling pastures.

She said of her mom and dad, "My parents raised me to never feel like I was entitled to success. That you have to work for it. You have to work so hard for it. And sometimes then you don't even get where you need to go."

It sounds like she's talking about having plenty of willitude! And if you study her career from a business standpoint, you'll see some tough navigotiating as well.

One more parting thought from Taylor Swift: "My parents taught me never to judge others based on whom they love, what color their skin is, or their religion."[6]

---

5 https://www.understood.org/en/articles/thanks-mom-quotes-from-celebrities-who-learn-and-think-differently
6 https://www.brainyquote.com/quotes/taylor_swift_579513

Measuring Your Value: Terry and Brandon

Alas, in our society, the most common way to measure your value to your community is by how much money you earn. The CEO is paid much more than the salesclerk. A leader of a big global corporation gets a bigger paycheck than the owner of a small neighborhood bistro. Someone who owns fifty apartment buildings receives more income than the person who owns one rental property.

But income and wealth aren't the *only* ways to measure how invaluable someone is, especially to themselves and to the people they serve. Personal significance is dimensional, including how we think, feel, believe, and act daily. Those four capacities add up to the personal significance expressed toward others, impacting how we influence those we interact with to become significant.

Here's a poignant example how a person can have what we call *intangible invaluableness*. You may not be able to measure it in tangible dollars or stock options, but it's nonetheless very powerful. So powerful, in fact, that it would be impossible to put a cash value on it.

Brandon was Terry's son with special needs. During his thirty-eight years of life that recently ended in a peaceful passing after a lengthy battle with a broken body that kept him in a quadriplegic condition from birth, he had great impact on the world. Brandon never spoke, walked, or fed himself, and he needed 24/7 care. His impact upon others, particularly those closest to him, was significant.

Terry writes:

My first marriage ended after twenty-two years of us serving him and even sleeping in three-hour shifts daily to care for him. That loss was not his fault but rather a failure on our part to reach out to professional care people before our marriage relationship ended. It took me several years to fully realize what I needed to do better, which was to reach out to invaluable persons or teams for more help without feeling shameful and regret. The flip side of that coin is that Brandon impacted thousands of people over the years, even through to today as I share our story of triumph over pain and brokenness through my writings and speaking events all over the world. Brandon changed my life forever as a person and a father. He taught me how to be calm and perform under pressure while helping him fight for life all those years while I was finding mine. I learned that my brokenness from not being able to heal him from his pain and suffering for almost four decades while grieving his eventual death gave me strength even in his passing!

Thank you, Brandon, for being "you" and helping me to understand how to care for myself and challenge others to become invaluable too. You can ask yourself, "What is broken in my life that I can convert into a dynamic impact on everyone I meet and know?" Becoming invaluable is a gift ready to be unwrapped through our service to others, investments in ourselves and others, and donations of time and money that will leave a legacy behind for others to reflect on and perhaps emulate themselves.

Here's one amazing moment. Once I learned to be proud of Brandon, I took him to a pre-race day. Emerson Fittapaldi, driving for Roger Penske, one of the top drivers and teams of that time, spotted Brandon. He came to him with great empathy and invited us to the pits on race day, which in turn started my opportunities to train race car drivers in the aspects of performance under tremendous stress or pressure, changing the trajectory of my career.

Here is another example. Giving birth to a child and being an attentive mother, and then raising that child to adulthood in a successful fashion, either as her mother, father, or other caregiver, is a vocation of love that puts you in a position to be invaluable in the development of a person. And even in this incredibly important role of the development of a child, a mother, father, or other caregiver can apply the approach within this book to continuously improve in this vital role.

There are some other types of people who are invaluable to their communities and yet who do not earn top incomes. These may include non-profit leaders and volunteers at the local hospital or women's shelter, or people who coach little league sports, or who work in the local food pantry. Doctors who spend their vacations volunteering in developing nations don't get paid and yet are absolutely invaluable to the impoverished regions they serve. Artists often make strong contributions to the world without much compensation. As mentioned, Vincent van Gogh made some of the most influential and important art in our history, and yet he lived in poverty. His brother Theo bought him his art supplies, and he sold only one or two paintings in his lifetime, but after his death he became an invaluable part of our culture.

The number one criterion, and the only one that truly matters, is your happiness with your life. If you are happy to follow in the steps of Mother Theresa and serve the poor with no thought of enriching yourself, then make that your life's purpose, vision, and mission. If that's your path, this book will be useful to you because the fundamental principles we present are valid for anyone who seeks to become invaluable with or without the economic value.

Having said that, if you're in the world of business, commerce, or popular entertainment, which means you're working for money, it's safe to say if you find your passion and follow it, then your value, as measured by how much money you make, has nowhere to go but up. How much you're paid in the job market is just one tangible aspect of human activity, but we use it as a yardstick because it's easy to measure. We can easily say, "The fryolator guy is paid a tiny fraction of the what the CEO gets, and therefore he's less valuable to the company." In our industrialized society, this is true. And it's also true that the fryolator guy and the CEO are replaceable. But the cost of replacing the CEO is much higher, and he or she is presumed to possess knowledge, skills, and experience that are uncommon.

In the pages ahead, we'll talk much more about these three key human attributes.

Your happiness depends on how you define success. And because this is a practical book about how to support yourself and your family over the course of your career, we're going to assume that you're a working member of your community, you need to pay your bills, and you need financial and job security. You don't want to just survive; you want to be *on top in your vocation of choosing*. You are or want to be passionate about what you do, want to be the decision-maker, the person who signs the paychecks, and the one who charts the course for the organization or for yourself. You want to be the one to whom others turn for advice, and you want to be well compensated for that advice. You want to be influential and your opinion well respected.

Supply and Demand Are Key

There's one more thing about being invaluable that we need to understand: your tangible value to your community depends on context and the relationship between supply and demand.

Here is what we mean. Let's say you're really good at making pizza. You know every recipe and nuance of pizza making. However, you live in a neighborhood in a big city where there's a pizza parlor on every block. Everyone knows how to make pizza. Grandmas, grandpas, sons, daughters—they all know how to make killer pizza. In this context, are your skills invaluable? No, they're not! You are just one person among thousands with a commonplace ability. You have nothing to offer that's unique. You cannot command a top wage because, while the demand exists, the supply is plentiful.

Then you decide to move to a city where pizza is not readily available. Good pizza parlors do not exist. You open your pizza shop, and people are amazed. They have never had such good pizza! Soon, you find that when it comes to pizza, you are invaluable. You are the king of pizza in your town. You have become invaluable because you have a rare and coveted skill, and people will pay you handsomely for it. The demand exists, and you're the only source of supply.

To be invaluable in the first city would require you to create something truly new and different in the world of pizza that would shift the demand, allowing you to become uniquely invaluable. Anything is possible, but what, where, and how you choose matters. It's all based on what you define as success with the consideration of the surrounding demand.

Let's look at one more scenario. Let's say you're an expert pizza maker and decide to leave your neighborhood where your skills are commonplace and move to a new city lacking in pizza parlors. You arrive and open your shop. But you find that you have no customers! Why not? Because in this particular city, the people have no interest in pizza. They do not know what it is and don't eat it. It means nothing to them. It has little value—and neither does your skill. Without demand, supply becomes irrelevant.

You realize that if you want to become invaluable as a pizza maker, you need to find an environment where the demand for your skill is high and the supply is low.

One more example. Let's say you are an expert fryolator repairman. In fact, you happen to be the only certified fryolator repairman within a hundred miles. This means that anytime a fryolator at a local fast-food or other restaurant breaks down, the location manager can call only one person: you. When you get the call, you can pretty much name your price, because your services are in high demand and the supply of fryolator repairmen is very low. At that moment, you are invaluable!

Logically, this is the takeaway. The knowledge, skills, and experience that are invaluable are those that are the most difficult and are in high demand. Let's consider what's probably the most challenging job in America, getting elected president of the United States. The skill required is easy to describe. You need to persuade seventy million or more of your fellow citizens to proactively cast a vote for you. You need to capture enough votes to win the Electoral College. This is a job very few people have the ability to perform, and it's made more exclusive by the fact that only one person can be president, and then after four years you have to reapply. The skills required are extraordinary, and the demand for someone to fill the position is extremely high.

The Hermès Birkin Bag

Here's a revealing story about supply and demand and being invaluable. It comes from Hermès, the French luxury design house established in 1837. When the company introduced the hand-crafted Birkin handbag in 1984, it was an immediate sensation. Despite—or perhaps because of—the five-figure price tag, the company had to create a waiting list of up to six years until you could purchase a Birkin bag or its cousin, the Kelly bag. When you finally received the coveted call notifying you that a bag was available, it may have been in a very different color of leather, hardware, or size than you requested. Yet, woe betide the woman who held out for the bag she really wanted! She was unlikely to receive a second call.

So how can you buy a Birkin bag? People who know about these things say it's all about your personal relationship with one of the roughly three hundred Hermès stores worldwide. The bottom line is that the more you spend on *other stuff* at Hermès, like luggage or jewelry, the higher on the list you'll go. And the more you get to know a sales associate, the greater your chances become that the sales associate will say, "As long as you're buying this lovely watch for fifty thousand dollars, allow me to mention that we just happen to have a Birkin bag in stock. Would you care to see it?"

In a nutshell, because of its relentless pursuit of quality and luxury, to ultra-wealthy women Hermès has made itself an invaluable brand of handbags. The bags are truly coveted. And if you make yourself an invaluable customer of Hermès by spending lavishly at their stores, you'll be on the VIP list of customers who have the opportunity to buy one. One hand washes the other, so to speak.

We must also consider the element of competition and change. In our world, nothing stays the same for very long. Technological innovation is accelerating. How businesses are operated is changing. The marketplace is evolving. A person in business in 1980 who gets magically transported across time to the present day would be amazed and bewildered by the changes that have taken place. This matters because the personal assets that make you invaluable today will probably not make you invaluable tomorrow. The world is full of occupations that were robust years ago but today are disappearing or don't even exist: Telephone operators (remember them?), watch and clock repairmen, door-to-door salespeople, admin assistants, telemarketers, bank tellers, shoe repairmen. Knowledge and skill requirements of existing jobs are constantly changing, as well as the one you are striving to be in one day. Anyone in the tech industry knows that you need to constantly update your proficiency or risk falling behind. Today, standing still or resting on your laurels is not an option. To stay invaluable, you need to keep moving forward, advancing your knowledge and skills as well as the vision you have for yourself in life.

You Determine Your Own Path: Steve on the Plane

There's no road map for life! Just when you think you know where you're going, some person or circumstance will place a boulder in the road, or offer you the chance to choose another road. By developing the ability to navigate and negotiate—which we'll talk much more about in the pages ahead—you'll be able to confidently create your own path to an invaluable mindset. In succeeding chapters, you'll learn how to put these concepts into practice through examples from our own and others' careers and life experiences.

We hope you think of these principles as being not just about career or business-based guidelines but applicable to any life experience. We live our best lives when we've attained an invaluable mindset.

Here's an example from Steve's personal experience.From one fateful airplane trip from New Jersey to Dallas, a cascade of events happened in my life that changed it forever. As I look back now, I can see the significance of one opportunity and its tremendous effects on my life. At the time, I was less than a year out of college and, after nine months of training, about to be deployed into a sales position in the Commodity Chemical Division of Diamond Shamrock, a major regional refiner and marketer of petroleum products and natural gas. It was a major opportunity for me coming out of college—at least on paper.

Aboard this flight, I met the head of training and the national sales manager of Corning Medical. We had an eye-open-ing discussion. And just three weeks after that fateful flight, thanks to my chance introduction to these two top executives at the company, I found myself going to work in sales for Corning Medical. There, I was perceived with high value, and this was the first of many steps over the past four decades to becoming invaluable. This change opened the door to many other advances in life. I met my beautiful wife, Deb, after Corning acquired Gilford Instruments. Additionally, as a result of going through some external sales training provided by Corning Medical, the training was repeated and advanced over five years by the same outside firm, leading to my first opportunity in consulting with Sales Development Associates. This experience was influential in the balance of my career, as my sales and marketing skills developed significantly over the next five years.

Not all elements of the steppingstones in developing knowledge, skills, and experience are necessarily positive. In fact, two of my next three opportunities in senior leadership positions ended in two major failures in my career progression. The key was to learn and develop resiliency and the ability to recover quickly and move forward. I recovered from these failures with greater knowledge, skill, experience, and resiliency. All of these events contributed to the outcome years later that I've built and sold a very successful consulting firm.

This chance encounter on the airplane resulted in a positive outcome because Steve was open-minded about making changes to the path he was on. His life had a certain trajectory that seemed to be sufficient. But a new opportunity presented itself, and instead of being locked into a single course, Steve was flexible and recognized that another path, which he had not previously considered, was an important next step to achieve his vision of success.

Everyone brings value to a relationship, organization, and career. The question is how one becomes invaluable or indispensable in whatever role one is involved in through life? What it takes to become invaluable is an understanding of oneself from a health, strength, and worth perspective to develop the commitment and related habits that lead to being invaluable.

The interesting part of knowing oneself is that most people spend much of their time worrying about what others think of them, thereby wasting time on trivial matters, versus focusing yourself on the most important aspects of being a person of health, body and mind, strength, character and resiliency, and thereby developing your own self-worth.

The challenge for most of us is to learn who we are and what we are good at and then set off in our lives to achieve what we can with a supporting approach to help create flexibility and resiliency for ourselves to develop invaluableness, making us nearly irreplaceable. We hope you will discover how our approach and methodology, when applied with real commitment, will catapult your invaluableness.

The Desire to Learn

To become invaluable—and stay that way through technological disruption and a rapidly changing culture—you need to *keep learning*, adding to your knowledge, skills, and experience. It's a very simple formula.

You keep learning = continued success.

You stop learning = stagnation and failure.

Consider Warren Buffett, who in the world of investing has been invaluable for many decades. He's so revered that students of investing call him "The Oracle of Omaha" and eagerly devour his annual letters to his Berkshire Hathaway investors. Each year, Buffett presides over Berkshire Hathaway's annual shareholder meeting, an event drawing over 20,000 visitors from both the United States and abroad, giving it the nickname "Woodstock of Capitalism." When he was ninety years old—two decades or more beyond when many people have retired and are playing pickleball in Florida or Arizona—Buffett was still deeply involved in his business. His secret for continued success? He's a voracious reader. As reported in Inc. magazine, "Buffett reportedly spends as much as six hours a day reading books. It may be a daunting prospect for most busy people, but if you're up to the task, the Oracle of Omaha advises that we read 500 pages every day. He says that's how *knowledge* works — it builds up like compound interest."

About his workday, Buffett has said, "I just sit in my office and read all day." He estimates that he spends eighty percent of his working day reading and thinking.

In *Working Together: Why Great Partnerships Succeed*, Buffett commented to author Michael Eisner about his long partnership with Charlie Munger, who shares his passion for lifelong learning:

"Look, my job is essentially just corralling more and more and more facts and information, and occasionally seeing whether that leads to some action. And Charlie—his children call him a book with legs."

Buffett reads with a goal. He wants to learn about new investing opportunities. He wants to become the expert on companies that are undervalued by the marketplace. These companies are what you might call the *invisibly invaluable*. They fly under the radar, delivering high value to their customers and investors, and yet are overlooked by the market. Buffett invests in them and then sits back and watches as they grow and thrive.

Speaking of reading and lifelong learning, one of the great readers of all time was the philanthropist Andrew Carnegie. An immigrant from Scotland, his career began in 1849 at the age of fourteen, when he became a telegraph messenger boy in the Pittsburgh Office of the Ohio Telegraph Company. His job was to run through the streets, delivering telegrams by hand to their various recipients. A hard worker, he memorized the locations of Pittsburgh's businesses and the faces of important men. But his grueling work schedule precluded any hope of attending school.

Carnegie's opportunity for education and self-improvement came when he was given access to a magnificent library. As Carnegie himself wrote, "Colonel James Anderson—I bless his name as I write—announced that he would open his library of four hundred volumes to boys, so that any young man could take out, each Saturday afternoon, a book which could be exchanged for another on the succeeding Saturday.... The windows were opened in the walls of my dungeon through which the light of *knowledge* streamed in. Every day's toil and even the long hours of night service were lightened by the book which I carried about with me and read in the intervals that could be snatched from duty. And the future was made bright by the thought that when Saturday came, a new volume could be obtained."

To young Andrew Carnegie, Colonel James Anderson was an invaluable person.

Andrew Carnegie became a powerful business tycoon, but he always remembered the people who had helped him and the value of the gift of reading. In 1901, at the age of sixty-six, Carnegie sold his steel company and dedicated the remainder of his life to philanthropy. Before his death in 1919, Carnegie gave away over $350 million (that's about $10 billion today) to a vast array of charitable projects, with a special focus on building public libraries. Eventually, a total of 2,509 Carnegie libraries were built between 1883 and 1929 in the United States and around the world. Two quotes attributed to Carnegie sum up his belief in the power of reading.

"A library outranks any other one thing a community can do to benefit its people. It is a never failing spring in the desert."

"There is not such a cradle of democracy upon the earth as the Free Public Library, this republic of letters, where neither rank, office, nor wealth receives the slightest consideration."

Andrew Carnegie was truly invaluable—not just as a business leader but as a promotor of literacy and learning. Gaining knowledge continuously about businesses, your occupation or vocation through reading is the foundation of knowledge and skills.

We would propose both Buffett and Carnegie would agree, through technology many different modalities of learning are open to us to enhance our learning. From written books, audio books, podcasts, YouTube, Ted Talks, etc., so much is available as resources for learning. Think of it this way; If news around the world can be broadcast across the global in hundreds of languages in a matter of minutes from the time an incident occurs, any one with internet access can learn about whatever their hearts and minds desire at a moments notice.

Below is a quick reminder of the visual we will refer to throughout the book

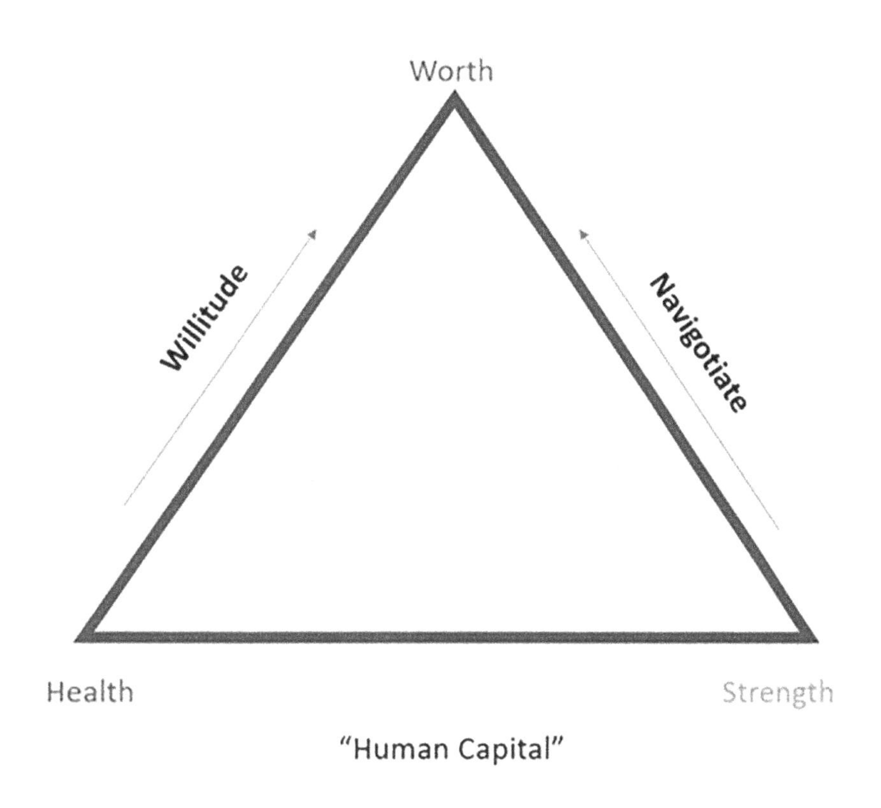

Invaluable Spotlight Profile: Tim Mitchell

Tim Mitchell grew up the descendant of two very prominent physicians in Michigan where his father and grandfather both practiced. The expectation was Tim would be the third-generation physician. Tim had other plans given his love of the guitar. After browsing through the Guitar Player Magazine and realizing that one of his heroes, Pat Martinez, had dropped out of school at fifteen and never looked back caused Tim to consider doing the same. Knowing quitting school was out of the question for himself as well as his parents, Tim enrolled into the School of Arts in Northern Michigan. While he enjoyed a short stay at the Northern Michigan the lack of a guitar program led Tim to the University of Miami.

While at University of Miami, considered one of the top programs in music, Tim pushed himself on the guitar every day to develop the skills that opened doors! Tim auditioned for Barry Manilow, which was successful. Once winning the position with Manilow he received a call that Bob Seger was interested for him to come to do a music video with Bob Seger & The Silver Bullett Band. Things were moving along in Tim's career, all his effort was paying off as he continued to be perceived with greater and greater value in the music industry. One of the biggest opportunities resulted from a trip back to LA when, a friend of his from school called him about an opportunity with Gloria Estefan. Tim went on to perform with her at Madison Square Garden and was later introduced to Shakira. Tim was invited on tour with Shakira in Latin America and once she launched into the English market, Tim wrote music for some of her top hits, including a number one hit. Tim's invaluableness was now at the top in the music world. Failure was never an option, always pushing to be the best. When looking back, Tim feels very fortunate to have done as well as he has and the journey never seemed like a difficult task, just natural.

Tim, as a result of his success, had other opportunities though he decided to stay with Shakira and continues his work with her today. Looking back Tim's view was "failure was not an option", and when you have no other way to make it in life and nothing else to fall back on, you simply must dedicate yourself twenty four hours a day, every day, to simply "do it" and that is success! Becoming Invaluable is commitment to excellence to become the very best at what you do and in Tim's case to write and play music with the best.

THE BOTTOM LINE!

- Explore how you can become invaluable to your family, business, community, or even just one person.
- Pathways to becoming invaluable include:

  Invent, make, or sell something of value
  Provide a valuable service
  Civic or business leadership
  Moral or spiritual leadership
  Science
  Teacher
  Arts and entertainment
  Being invaluable to one person

- Income and wealth aren't the only ways to measure how invaluable someone is. Personal significance is dimensional, including how we think, feel, believe, and act daily.
- Your tangible value to your community depends on context and the relationship between supply and demand. The knowledge, skills, and experience that are invaluable are those that are the most difficult and are in high demand.
- To become invaluable—and stay that way through technological disruption and a rapidly changing culture—you need to *keep learning*, adding to your knowledge, skills, and experience.
- Reading, listening to Audio Books, Podcasts all enhance your learning and can add to your knowledge and skills.

WILLITUDE AND NAVIGOTIATE

We will develop throughout this book the importance of the five personal attributes—knowledge, skills, and attitude, as well as health and strength—and more, so let's dive into two more personal assets you must develop to become truly invaluable to your workplace, your community, and your family. Then we will build out the foundational attributes of how you develop willitude and navigotiation in your life.

Willitude

The first thing you need to develop is your *willitude.*

What's willitude?

Put simply, it's a combination of willpower and fortitude.

Willpower can be defined as the ability to delay gratification and resist short-term temptations in order to meet long-term goals. It's the capacity to override an unwanted thought, feeling, or impulse. You find it commonly in self-improvement activities, such as dieting to lose weight: "I won't eat that piece of chocolate cake because I'm trying to take off ten pounds. I will use my willpower to resist temptation."

Fortitude is the strength of mind that enables a person to encounter danger or bear pain or adversity with courage. It comes from the Latin word "*fortis*," meaning "strong," and while it once included physical strength, now it's used principally for mental toughness. As we work to become invaluable, we will address the physical aspects of health and strength that help you develop a healthy brain through a strong body, developing greater fortitude. We can say: "She showed her fortitude by earning her college degree while working full time as a server in a restaurant and taking care of her elderly mother."

Your journey to being invaluable starts with the foundation of health and strength. They help build the personal quality we call *willitude*, which requires a fully developed sense of resilience and mental toughness. You can think of it as grit with a healthy intellectual and emotional base.

Willitude takes a tremendous amount of fortitude, and not just in the context of the business world. To be successful in whatever you do, you need to stay committed and keep improving as you move through periods of plateauing or challenge. It is the attitudinal will to succeed in your area of focus and developed expertise, which helps build success.

Having willitude does *not* mean you're rigid and unwilling to adapt as conditions change. In fact, quite the opposite is true. True mental toughness requires an instinctive flexibility, because without flexibility there is no growth, and without growth willitude becomes mere stubbornness and implacability. You'll quickly become stuck.

Willitude has nothing to do with your current station in life. Everybody has to begin somewhere, and we all start at different places in our lives. Some start early—by the time he was seventeen years old, Bill Gates was dabbling in the computer industry, and at the age of twenty he dropped out of school to launch Microsoft. In contrast, Colonel Harland Sanders was sixty-two when he opened the first Kentucky Fried Chicken franchise in South Lake, Utah. Sculptor Louise Bourgeois was in her seventies when her art was first recognized by New York museums.

Some people aren't sure what path they want to take in life, and so they try various careers. That's fine! If you keep at it, eventually you'll find what you were meant to do, what truly fulfills the purpose behind your passion in life. President Ronald Reagan didn't enter politics until he was fifty-three years old. This was in 1964 when he volunteered to give a speech in support of Barry Goldwater, who was then running for president. In 1966, Reagan—the former actor and president of the Screen Actors Guild union—was elected governor of California. He was nearly seventy years old when he became president of the United States in January, 1981.

Many people dutifully endure the lousy circumstances that life has handed them. They go to school and then get a job—any job—to pay the bills and launch a career. At some point they say, "Enough!" and summon the willitude to break free and make their own way in the world. Their change of life may or may not involve a higher paycheck. A person can come from a background of poverty or wealth yet face the same challenge of establishing one's own path in life, breaking free from the strife of their circumstances. Here's a question to ask.

Is it better to be a well-paid bookkeeper on Wall Street or an invaluable forest ranger in a national park?

Is it better to be a deckhand on a giant cruise ship or the captain of your own charter yacht?

Is it better to be a copywriter for a big city newspaper or a self-employed career novelist like Stephen King?

Is it better to work on the assembly line in a sprawling factory or to own your own niche manufacturing company?

These are questions only you can answer. But in each case, in the first choice your market value is very low, while in the second choice you're becoming invaluable in your world.

Some people climb their way slowly and patiently up the corporate ladder, increasing their value with each step. Consider Mary Barra, who in 2014 became the first female leader of a major global automaker. Her journey to the top had been a long one. At age eighteen, she got a summer job at General Motors, checking fender panels and inspecting hoods at a Pontiac plant. The money she made helped pay for her college tuition at General Motors Institute, now called Kettering University, in Flint, Michigan. Her job marketplace value at that time? Not very much! In 1985, she graduated from the institute with a degree in electrical engineering and started work as a senior engineer at a Pontiac Fiero plant. Her bosses sent her to Stanford Business School, and immediately after getting her MBA her increased value landed her a job as a GM manager, running manufacturing planning.

More promotions followed. She served as general director of internal communications and then manager of the Detroit/Hamtramck plant with its 3,400 employees, a major step forward in her career. Showing her willitude and as you will see next her navigotiation, she moved to increasingly important jobs in manufacturing engineering, including head of global human resources during GM's bankruptcy period from 2009 to 2011.

In 2013 she stepped up to executive vice president-global product development, purchasing, and supply chain. In January 2014, Mary Barra was named chief executive of General Motors and the first female head of an auto company.

She used her value and influence to change GM's notorious bureaucracy and put a new focus on results. One of her most well-known statements was this simple edict: "No more crappy cars." She threw out the massive, detailed company dress code and replaced it with two words: "Dress appropriately."

She quickly became one of the highest paid auto executives in America, and regularly appeared at the top of the "Most Powerful Women" lists published by *Forbes* and *Fortune* magazines. Had she shown both willpower and fortitude? Yes! Had she become invaluable? Absolutely!

We all have different career goals that may or may not be based on financial success. The key is having a feeling of self-worth. Without a feeling that we are doing something that fulfills us and not just fills our bank account, our success will feel hollow, if it's attained at all. This book is written to assist people in any walk of life to achieve that full sense of self-worth as one is *Becoming Invaluable!*

Navigotiate

The second word we're going to use often is *navigotiate*. This is a combination of navigate and negotiate, and it's a priceless skill.

To *navigate* has nautical roots and means to plan and direct the route or course of a ship, especially by using instruments, maps, or other way-finding tools. The word has evolved to mean, to make your way through a route that may have obstacles, such as the football player who navigates his way through the opposing players for the touchdown. And it's used in the computer industry, to move from one accessible page, section, or view of a file or website to another. For example, you might say: "This website is easy to navigate. I can find any page quickly!"

The word *negotiate* means to get a mutually agreeable result by the process of discussion. It's when you try to reach an agreement or compromise by talking or communicating with others. In business it happens often. "To produce our product, the vendor wants to charge us ten dollars per unit, while we think it should be eight dollars. But if we negotiate, we can come to an agreement."

Why do we need both words to form navigotiate? Think of a downhill skier who needs to navigate his way through the space between two trees. The trees are inanimate objects. They don't move, and you can't talk to them. So all the energy and effort is expended by the skier.

That's not how business works, because businesses are owned and operated by people, and people aren't trees. To resolve an issue and move ahead, you need both sets of skills. In human interactions, you need your navigational skills to know the relevant facts and figures and determine your best choices.

You need to know, for example, that another vendor will produce the product for eight dollars per unit, but their quality is suspect. With the right vendor, you could go as high as nine dollars per unit if shipping costs are kept low.

You also need your negotiating skills in order to interact with your counterpart and arrive at the best deal possible. The underlying skills of effective communication require knowledge and skill around listening, questioning, and adapting to different styles of people. All of our skills are necessary to negotiate tricky situations and complex human beliefs.

A key part of navigotiate is resilience, which means being able to hit an obstacle, bounce off it, and then keep going toward your goal. Resilience is important not just for dealing with obstacles but also to maximize opportunities. Mastering the art of navigotiating gives you the confidence to go into any situation you encounter. Later in the book, we'll expand upon some related skills helpful to navigotiating your way with regards to people.

Not succumbing to fear is an important part of this process. It's been said that seventy percent of the people in the world move away from challenges while thirty percent of the people in the world move toward challenges. You want to have the confidence it takes to move toward challenges and the wisdom to know how to get the most from the opportunity.

The foundation of willitude and navigotiate are two key personal attributes that you need to continuously develop in order to maximize your capabilities. Meanwhile, knowledge, skills, and attitude combined with health and strength are aspects one must continuously work on as one is *Becoming Invaluable!* Before we can focus on these five attributes one must also develop an understanding of defining our purpose in life and the values (principles or standards) by which we will conduct ourselves throughout our life.

Invaluable Spotlight Profile: Dan Clark

Dan Clark is a renowned motivational speaker, author, and CEO of Clark Success Systems. But his path to becoming invaluable wasn't always clear—he had to discover it.

In high school and college, Dan seemed destined to be a professional athlete. He was the projected #1 draft pick by the Oakland Raiders when he suffered a spinal injury that left him paralyzed for fourteen months. While recovering, he gave his first motivational speech ... and realized he had a new calling.

He came to believe his football accident was the best thing that had ever happened to him—not because of the injury but because of who he became because of it.

He met Zig Ziglar, who changed his life and personally mentored him for twenty-five years in the art and science of speaking, writing, and storytelling. In 1982, Dan was named an Outstanding Young Man of America and was sponsored by Ziglar into the National Speakers Association. Dan quickly became one of the most sought-after speakers in North America, and was honored by President Ronald Reagan with the Presidential Service Award as the primary speaker for Mrs. Nancy Reagan's "Just Say No" program.

Ziglar taught him what makes a person invaluable: "Wealth flows *through* you, not *to* you!

Dan's advice? "We all need to let go of the people in our lives who keep dragging us into the past."

THE BOTTOM LINE!

- Begin to develop two key personal attributes that you need to become invaluable: your willitude and your ability to navigotiate.
- Willitude is the powerful combination of willpower and fortitude. It does not mean you're rigid and unwilling to adapt as conditions change. True mental toughness requires an instinctive flexibility, because without flexibility there is no growth, and without growth willitude becomes mere stubbornness and implacability.
- Navigotiate is the combination of navigate and negotiate. In human interactions, you need your navigational skills to know the relevant facts and figures and to determine your best choices. You also need your negotiating skills in order to interact with your counterpart and arrive at the best deal possible.

PURPOSE AND VALUES: THE BEDROCK SUPPORTING THE FOUNDATION OF HEALTH AND STRENGTH

In the previous chapter, we introduced the important concepts of willitude and navigotiate. To develop these two key capabilities and make a difference in the world, you should strive to understand and build the five key attributes to develop both a sound mind and a sound body. More on developing your mind and body just ahead.

The tools you possess require a passion and emotion or, as you will see, true inspiration to direct them. There is no guidebook that tells you what you must do with your life and the opportunities you have. We have ancient and modern moral and spiritual guides, such as the Bible, to which you can turn for additional guidance. We also have civil laws that prohibit certain activities. For example, becoming a successful scam artist and stealing people's money is an activity frowned upon by both the Bible and by human laws. Such people are definitely not invaluable to anyone except themselves. In contrast, being a doctor, inventor, artist, or business leader are a few of the many activities which our society looks upon with favor and can consider to be invaluable.

But here's the best news. How you make yourself invaluable is no one's decision but your own. You need to find your own path, even if you're blazing it for the first time! If you find yourself in unfamiliar territory, your achievement will be that much more notable.

For example, when Jeff Bezos walked away from his lucrative Wall Street job in 1994 and drove to Seattle to start his crazy internet bookstore, he was forging a new path. He told his investors—the few he could convince to back him, including his parents—that the odds were great they would all lose their money. In fact, he gave his new venture only a thirty percent chance of success. He had no guidebook to rely on. He had to write the guidebook! And today, few could deny that Amazon.com is invaluable in many ways.

Bezos succeeded for several reasons. He had a really good business idea. He had as much knowledge, skills, and attitude that anyone in the internet retail industry could at the time. He also had the four key attributes that made his success possible: a purpose, values, a vision, and a mission.

Purpose

Imagine you're walking along and see a man sitting in a booth or stall by the side of the road. On the booth is a big sign saying, "NEW INVENTION FOR SALE! ONLY $100." Sure enough, in the booth he's displaying a complicated contraption.

When you meet him, you say to him, "I couldn't help but notice your interesting device! It must be very useful! What does it do? What's its purpose?"

"Its purpose?" says the man.

"Yes! It looks very sophisticated, as if a tremendous amount of knowledge and skill went into its design and construction! What's it for?"

The man looks at you with a blank expression. "I'm sorry," he says. "It has no purpose. It just is."

"No purpose? It does absolutely nothing for people? It doesn't even entertain them. It's not a work of art?"

The man nods. "Correct. No purpose. But it's new."

"Well then," you reply, "even though it's complicated in appearance, because it has no purpose, it has no value to me. Thank you and have a nice day." Such a device would cause you to wonder about the inspiration or motivation to bring such a worthless thing into existence.It's easy to talk about physical objects as having a purpose and having little or no value if they have no purpose. Human beings are more of a challenge, because you can argue that a human being does not need a purpose to be valued. A human being can choose to go off and live a solitary life in the forest, producing nothing of value to anyone else, and in the eyes of God that person is a priceless creation. According to many scholars, the Bible is clear that the ultimate purpose of man (humanity) is to glorify God, as it is written in Isaiah:

"Everyone who is called by my name, whom I have created for my glory; I have formed him, yes, I have made him." (Isaiah 43:7)

We mention this as a starting point of the discussion, and from there we can assert that, having created us, God must want us to survive and thrive on earth. To do this, we need to work cooperatively. Unlike many other animals, humans cannot long survive in nature outside of the group. We *must* work together. But to have every human possess exactly the same skills would be highly inefficient. We succeed when each of us has his or her own specialization or purpose in life and we combine our individual purposes to benefit the whole. For example (to put it simplistically), an individual can be a dentist, doctor, engineer, artist, soldier, farmer, entertainer—any one of a multitude of specializations. When we put these various skills all together, we succeed.

To be a valuable member of society is good. To be invaluable is better because your contribution to the group is that much greater.

Your purpose is a key factor in your becoming invaluable. Your purpose is the mast around which everything revolves, the anchor, the compass that helps guide you through the diversity of life.

Then what's a purpose? Purpose is the "why" to what we are endeavoring to achieve in life! Purpose is the driving fuel source to make anything possible that will align with all the other mechanics and formulas for success.

Purpose is both external and internal in nature.

External influence (motivation) can come from various places around us, but motivation is limited by that force to continually push us forward from other people, places, and things.

Internal influence (inspiration) comes from within and needs nothing from the external influence to fuel optimal results.

So what is the difference between motivation and inspiration?

Motivation is external and inspiration is internal.

Motivation is a sort of life support system that needs external influence to exist, but inspiration is the natural human wiring that was gifted to us as infants for the first time from the separation of womb and umbilical cord from our mothers. Inspiration is breath to our physical bodies that empowers all human life function. After birth, we breathe (inspire) our physical system, detached from our mother's womb support system.

A motivated person needs external support to exist, while the inspired person is self-empowered to claim and experience all of life's dreams, goals, and aspirations.

To further explore the definition of purpose, let's start very simplistically with machines and tools.

The purpose of a hammer is to assist humans with driving nails into wood. We do this to build houses, which provide shelter for people. This is the benefit of a hammer.

The purpose of an MRI machine is to provide images of your organs, tissues, and skeletal system without invasively harming you. We use these machines to help doctors diagnose and treat diseases so that you can stay healthy. This is the benefit of an MRI machine.

Okay, how about people?

The purpose of a firefighter is to save lives while putting out fires in people's homes or businesses and help keep them safe. This is the benefit to us of a firefighter.

The purpose of a farmer is to help feed the population by growing food for people. This is the benefit to us of a farmer.

Okay, let's say you decide, as a human being, to go live on a mountaintop, alone, without interaction with other humans. You make nothing and help no one. Of course, as a free person and child of God, you have every right to do this. Your life is priceless no matter where you are. If you fell off the mountain and got injured, people—even strangers—would try to help you.

But you're not invaluable because you have no purpose in life that relates to helping other people be happy or healthy. This matters to human society because tens of thousands of years ago, when we were hunter-gatherers living day-to-day off the land, we figured out that *we needed each other to survive.* This is no joke. A lone human out in the wilderness wouldn't last long against big, powerful predators thousands of years ago. As a species, we're fairly weak physically, and our key advantage lies in the fact that we're smart, social, and know how to work cooperatively. Eons ago, we discovered the value of a division of labor and specialization. We could plan together and outsmart our sharp-toothed adversaries. The most invaluable member of the tribe was the person with wisdom and leadership abilities who could lead the group to safety or hunt down food sources.

Thousands of years later, we're still a highly collaborative species. We contribute our talents to achieve a common goal, whether that be putting a man on the moon or getting the kids to school on time. The people among us who we consider to be invaluable are those with a clear purpose in life, and that purpose is to do something that benefits the group as a whole. In the United States, we generally consider the most invaluable person to be the president, and especially so if he or she is the leader of your party. There are many other invaluable people—business leaders, artists, dedicated mothers or fathers, politicians, athletes, teachers—in various sectors of our society. You'll notice that we generally characterize invaluable people by their occupation, or by the role they play in the economy and society.

Establishing your purpose in life is no easy task. It is from the internal perspective of finding your inspiration by answering a question. Why do I exist? What inspires me to achieve invaluable outcomes in my life? Earlier we shared that for Steve it is to provide and care for his family. For Terry, it is to influence and help others perform even under great stress or pressure. Discovering your purpose in life may happen at an early or later age. Our desire is to help you define your purpose, one that will align your focus, regardless of obstacles you may encounter, to inspire yourself to have the willitude to achieve invaluableness.

Purpose on its own may not provide you with all the foundational bedrock you need in life by itself. The foundation necessary to support yourself through thick and thin, through virtuous moments and to be scrupulous when encountering illicit situations, requires values along with your purpose. To strengthen our purpose we need to determine the three to five values by which we will conduct ourselves throughout our career and chosen life or vocation.

As an example, a value chosen by Steve is character. Steve defines character as: "Doing the right thing even when no one else is looking." Character includes honesty, trust, and integrity. Steve arrived at this definition for himself through his belief that someone, God in his view, is always looking. In addition to character, he operates with four other principles or behaviors that guide him in his actions and decisions.

Putting these values to work in conjunction with his purpose to provide and care for his family, Steve enables himself to make excellent choices and stay on course to achieve not only his purpose but to reach his vision and accomplish the missions in life. We'll have more on vision and mission after we develop the five attributes necessary in becoming invaluable.

Your purpose and values combined become the foundational bedrock in how you will live your life and the pivot point around which your choices and decisions are determined. When you make well-aligned or appropriate decisions, good things tend to happen. If not, these poor choices do not bode well for becoming invaluable.

Values

While every person should have a purpose—especially if you are striving to become invaluable—it's only half of the equation.

The other half consists of your values.

What are values?

They are the principles that guide your purpose and give it direction.

Look at it this way. Your purpose is like a powerful engine that drives you forward. It propels you toward your goal. If you want to be a doctor, it gives you energy to do that. Whatever you want to do, it clarifies that in your mind and makes you say, "This is my purpose! I want to accomplish this!"

Here's the important part. Because we have God-given free will, it's possible for us to choose a purpose that's not in alignment with what we need to do to help our neighbors.

Let's be honest. People sometimes choose to harm others or themselves. They choose to enrich themselves unjustly or pursue unhealthy objectives.

In other words, as civilized people we recognize there are good purposes and bad purposes, and people can strive for either one (sometimes at the same time!). Of course, some people who are pursuing bad purposes will assert, "Well, what I'm doing is good for me!" But you get the idea—at the end of the day, we all know the difference between Mother Teresa and a criminal.

Your personal values act as the rudder of your ship or the steering wheel of your car. They determine the direction of your purpose. They are your central beliefs and the tenets that guide your actions, influence your behavior, inform your decision-making, and govern your relationships with loved ones.

Your values can lead you through success and challenging times, giving you strength when you need it to accomplish your purpose despite adversity.

As Alexander Hamilton said, "If you don't stand for something, you will fall for anything."

The importance of your values is that they tell you what you stand for.

While your values are likely to be constant throughout your life, your purpose may change or evolve. When you're young, your overriding purpose may be to establish yourself in business and care for your family. Thirty years later, when the kids are grown and you're nearing retirement age, your purpose may shift to helping your community as a philanthropic donor and board member of charitable organizations.

This is exactly what Andrew Carnegie, arguably America's greatest philanthropist, did. He spent the first sixty-six years of his life in the steel industry, building one of the world's greatest fortunes. Then in 1901 he sold the business for an amount equal to $10 billion today, which he added to his existing fortune. From that day until his death eighteen years later, he gave away his money by funding hundreds of philanthropic initiatives. Most notable were the Carnegie libraries, which he helped build in three thousand locations in the United States and around the world. He literally couldn't give away his money fast enough, and when he died in 1919, he left an estate valued at thirty million dollars to various foundations, charities, and pensioners.

The "Andrew Carnegie Dictum" was:

- To spend the first third of one's life getting all the education one can.
- To spend the next third making all the money one can.
- To spend the last third giving it all away for worthwhile causes.

While Carnegie's purpose in life evolved, his values never did. In 1868, at age thirty-three, he wrote: "The amassing of wealth is one of the worst species of idolatry. No idol is more debasing than the worship of money." Is this a contradiction to what he achieved by amassing money? It could have been, but the proof of his enduring values was the fact that he carried out his stated intentions.

What Are Values?

To me, your values should be your personal attributes that speak to how you relate to other people ethically and morally as you pursue your purpose. They can include:

- Honesty
- Integrity
- Kindness
- Empathy
- Wisdom
- Courage
- Respect
- Family

- Honor
- Accountability
- Teamwork
- Gratitude

There are many more! These are all positive values that will help make you invaluable to other people. In contrast, there are also some *negative values* that we know people have but which, in the long run, will *not* make them invaluable to their fellow human beings:

- Win at any cost
- Take advantage of someone weaker
- Lie when desirable for short-term gain
- Might makes right

You get the idea. I hope you don't have any of these values!

Where Do Our Values Come From?

We learn most of our values as children from our parents and extended families. We're taught by our parents, but even more powerfully we see what our parents actually *do*. If they preach honesty and then lie, we learn to do the same. If they are poor but hardworking and honest, we see that too. Our family values also spring from our social and cultural values. Sometimes new life experiences may influence values we previously held, such as when we go off to school and see kids and teachers behaving in a way we hadn't seen before.

If our family is religious, we get some of our values from going to church or the temple. But just like our family, we hope that the values professed by the church are the ones they act upon in everyday life so there's no contradiction. In the Judeo-Christian world, the first set of formal values we're exposed to are the Ten Commandments, which assert some basic tenets such as not to steal, to be honest, and not to be jealous of others. These have been shown to be extremely durable, and many of the principles contained in the Ten Commandments are fundamental to the Western legal tradition. Prohibitions on theft, murder, and perjury are found in nearly every legal code. In the realm of normative rules that order many societies, notions of respect for one's parents and admonitions against adultery are also implicit. Remember, in very ancient times, long before the Ten Commandments, the law was "every man for himself," and the strongest person could do whatever he wanted until someone stronger came along and dethroned him.

Your values should direct your purpose and the actions you take to achieve your purpose. If they do, then you'll feel good about yourself and the direction of your life. But if your values contradict what you're doing to fulfill your purpose, then you're going to feel tension and stress.

For example, if you sincerely value your relationship to your family, but you work seventy-hour weeks in your job and spend little time at home while your partner does all the "heavy lifting" with the family, you're going to feel internal stress and conflict. This is because your values don't align with your actions. Some people who find themselves in that situation may say, "I'm working seventy-hour weeks to make a good life for my family, which they will appreciate years from now." Maybe yes, maybe no. Only you can know in your heart if you're doing the right thing.

It can work the other way around. Let's say that competition is something you don't value. You prefer collaboration and cooperation among people for a common goal, but you're offered a job as a commissioned salesperson in a highly competitive environment. Will you be happy? Probably not. You can make a lot of money, but the nature of the job goes against your values.

In these types of situations, knowing your personal values can help. When you know *and follow* your own values, you can use them to make decisions about how to live your life, and you can answer questions like these:

What type of career should I pursue?

Should I accept a position with this company?

Should I follow family tradition or explore a new path?

Should I vote for this candidate?

Should I compromise with my neighbor or be resolute with my position?

Ideally, your values and your purpose will be in perfect alignment, offering you the opportunity to use your knowledge and skills to pursue your purpose. With your values and purpose working together, it'll be easy to have a positive attitude, and your powers of willitude and navigotiation will be in full play. Your health and strength will carry you through on your journey to becoming truly invaluable!

Invaluable Spotlight Profile: Maj. Gen (Ret.) John Gronski

Maj. Gen (Ret.) John Gronski is the founder and CEO of Leader Grove Consulting, LLC, a service-disabled veteran-owned business conducting leadership consulting, assessments, training, and executive coaching. The author of two bestselling books, *Iron-Sharpened Leadership* and *The Ride of Our Lives*, John develops and delivers keynote addresses, leadership workshops, presentations, team exercises, and group facilitations to global organizations.

An undistinguished student in school, his dad pushed him to consider a military career. John enlisted into the Army in 1978, loved it, and stayed until 1982.

In 1983 he and his wife began a bicycle ride across the United States, with John towing their fifteen-month-old son in a bike trailer. This was a defining period in his life, an incredible adventure and a memorable one.

He worked in the family business and then for a management consulting firm before returning to the military.

In 2019, after forty years of service in the Army, John retired as a two-star general. That's when he started his leadership consulting firm to help top executives improve their leadership ability.

John's advice on becoming invaluable includes:

- Know your purpose.
- Trust doesn't happen quickly—it takes time. You need to cultivate trust.

- Humility is an essential attribute for any leader, and unfortunately many leaders feel they don't need to be humble.

- Discover your own personal core values. John's core values are service, integrity, and respect. You need to live by your values, and your behaviors need to link to those values.

THE BOTTOM LINE!

- To survive on earth, humans must work together. We succeed only when each of us has his or her own purpose in life, and we combine our individual purposes to benefit the whole.
- Your purpose is a key factor in your becoming invaluable. Know your purpose—and use it to help yourself and others.
- Values are the principles that guide your purpose and give it direction. To strengthen your purpose, you need three to five values by which you'll conduct yourself throughout your life and chosen vocation.
- While your values are likely to be constant throughout your life, your purpose may change or evolve.
- Ideally, your values and your purpose will be in perfect alignment, offering you the opportunity to use your knowledge and skills to pursue your purpose, putting your powers of willitude and navigotiation in full play.

THE FIVE PERSONAL ATTRIBUTES

To become and stay invaluable is a good thing. It improves your life, enriches you, and gives you freedom to do what you want. But how do you elevate yourself from being just another face in the crowd to being invaluable to your family, community, or organization?

Let's develop how to do that with easy-to-understand steps. We're going to introduce some concepts and words that will be new to you, but don't worry. We'll make everything crystal clear.

First, let's talk about five personal attributes that you need to become invaluable. It would be difficult to imagine becoming invaluable, whether measured by your happiness, work compensation, or intangible value, without them. The five personal attributes in building your worth are knowledge, skills, attitude, health, and strength. Let's dive into each one.

1. Knowledge

The knowledge you have about the world or a subject or a skill set consists of the facts and information you've acquired through education, professional training, or experience. It's the theoretical or practical understanding of a subject. You have knowledge about a thing when you can describe its attributes, give a history of it, place it in context, or explain its advantages and defects.

For example, you can have extensive knowledge of the law. You may have a degree in law from a prestigious university, are able to cite important statutes, and can provide the history of various laws and legal traditions. You may also have knowledge of court procedures and how cases are tried.

The Seven Types of Knowledge

Let's begin with a qualification. We all know intuitively that there are many types of knowledge we acquire in different ways. If a bee stings you, you have acquired knowledge about the behavior of bees. If you read in a book that the Earth is ninety-three million miles from the Sun, that's another type of knowledge. If you add 2 + 2 and get 4, that's another type. If you go online and ask Google how many types of knowledge there are, you'll see that some people say there are four, six, or ten. No one can agree on an exact number! It's a subjective question, and there are many answers. For our purposes, we're going to stick with seven types. It's just our choice. We encourage you to think about the question and come up with your own answer.

Here are the seven types of knowledge collected by humans in our everyday lives. As you'll see, the definitions can be fluid and even overlapping. Don't think too deeply about them! Philosophers have been arguing about this stuff for centuries, and will probably keep arguing about it for centuries to come. But it's important to have a general grasp of the topic.

***A posteriori* knowledge.** We'll start with some Latin for you. *A posteriori* literally means "from the latter" or "from what follows." It's a term from logic that refers to reasoning that works backward from an effect to its causes. It depends on evidence, or warrant, from human sensory experience: something you can see, hear, touch, smell, or feel. *A posteriori* truth cannot be understood independently of reference to sensory experience. It's empirical, experience-based knowledge. Standard examples of *a posteriori* truths are the truths of ordinary perceptual experience, such as, "I see the tree in the forest," or "This water is cold."

A posteriori knowledge includes everyday conclusions you have drawn from your experience. For example, you could say, "Butterflies have two pairs of wings," because you've studied butterflies and have seen their wings. It also includes information you have received from others, such as, "The Eiffel Tower is in Paris, France." You may never have been to France, but you know this from the testimony of other people—what they say, what they've written, or their photographs of it.

***A priori* knowledge.** Here, the Latin means "from before" or "from the former." The 18th century philosopher Immanuel Kant popularized the contrasting ideas of "*a posteriori* knowledge" and "*a priori* knowledge" in his work *Critique of Pure Reason*. According to Kant, a proposition is *a priori* if it is both necessary and universal. A proposition is necessary if it could not possibly be false, and so cannot be denied without contradiction. In contrast, a proposition that is *a posteriori* does not convey universality and absolute necessity because there could be an exception.

A priori refers to knowledge a person has that they did not learn from their experiences. If a person can know that a given statement is true only by knowing the meaning of the words in the statement, or just by contemplating what the statement means, then it is an example of *a priori* knowledge. For example, "All horses are animals" is true, and a person can know that it is true because a definition of "horse" likely includes the fact that horses are animals. If you find a horse that is not an animal, then it's not a real horse.

Other examples would be, "A triangle has three sides," or "Two plus two equals four." These facts do not require sensory validation to be true.

Explicit knowledge. This is knowledge that can be documented, transmitted, and most importantly learned by outsiders. It's any information that's easy to share and understand, such as the operating instructions for a new product.

Explicit knowledge is stored in documents, books, libraries, films, photographs, audio files, and other forms of verbal or written communication. In business, it includes content that describes your product or service, training manuals, databases, reports, specifications, financial statements, contracts—any information or data that can be reproduced and distributed.

Implicit knowledge. This is often defined as the application of explicit knowledge. It's knowledge gained through the performance of everyday activities or without awareness that learning is occurring. Implicit knowledge can be taught, such as teaching someone how to use a computer.

Some examples of implicit knowledge are knowing how to walk, run, ride a bicycle, or play a musical instrument. In business, skills that are transferable from one job to another are one example of implicit knowledge. In other words, if you leave your job at Zenworks and go to work at General Electric, you'll bring with you implicit knowledge that you can immediately put to work in your new role.

Tacit knowledge. This is knowledge gained from personal experience that is more difficult to express and isn't easily taught. You can call it "learning by doing." When Malcolm Gladwell and others talked about needing ten thousand hours of practice to become proficient at a skill, that's tacit knowledge. When your business partner travels to China and successfully makes a deal to sell your products there, and he could do this because he had been to China many times, that's tacit knowledge. It would be difficult for him to teach you what he knows because so much of it depends upon how you respond to various situations. If you want to be invaluable, being able to tap into your tacit knowledge of a critical issue will put you in a good position.

Declarative knowledge. This is a subset of explicit knowledge. It comprises static information and facts that are specific to a given topic, which can be easily accessed and retrieved. This includes company rules and regulations as well as business goals. It also includes things like price lists or catalog entries. It's the type of knowledge that lends itself to comparisons, such as key performance metrics, a balance sheet, or the annual report.

Procedural knowledge. Another subset of explicit knowledge, this comprises *how* things are done. In business, it includes systems, such as how orders are processed or customer complaints handled. It's also how the law is applied, such as the procedures for going through an initial public offering or a stock split.

It's never too late to increase your knowledge! Many people have the ability to learn new information well into their senior years. For example, Priscilla Sitienei was a midwife from Nadat in rural Kenya. As a child, she had never learned to read or write. She lived her life as an illiterate, but at the age of eighty-seven she decided she wanted to become more invaluable to her family and community.

Along with six of her great-grandchildren, she enrolled at the Leaders Vision Preparatory School in Ndalat village of Nandi County, Kenya. Dressed in the standard school uniform of gray dress and green sweater, Sitienei said she went to class to set a good example for her great-grandchildren and to pursue a new career. "I would like to become a doctor because I used to be a midwife," she told Reuters, adding that her children were supportive of her decision.[7]

How do we measure knowledge? The traditional way is through formal education and the succession of academic degrees a person can earn in their lifetime, such as a high school diploma, associate degree, bachelor's degree, master's degree, and doctorate. There are also countless certificate and other non-degree programs that bolster lifelong learning. As we progress through school, we are trained to input knowledge using a host of methodologies. Reading, listening, watching, doing, and reviewing—they all culminate in testing, so that we may prove to both others and ourselves that we have absorbed the information. Professional certifications—in law, accounting, building, even hairdressing and manicuring—attest to the fact that we have the requisite knowledge to provide an acceptable level of service to others. Knowledge in a particular role, in your vocation, can be inventoried and accumulated.

---

7 Reuters. https://www.reuters.com/lifestyle/back-school-98-kenyan-woman-sets-example-next-generation-2022-02-09/

The funny thing about knowledge is that the more you know, the more you realize you *don't* know. As Socrates said, "To know is to know that you know nothing. That is the meaning of true knowledge." Our universe of knowledge is constantly expanding beyond our horizons. We humans will always make mistakes, but the more you know about a subject, the more likely it is that your mistakes will be small and inconsequential.

Here's the bottom line. Knowledge is the foundation upon which your skills and your attitude can build. You may have many skills and lots of positive attitude, but without knowledge of your subject you cannot hope to create anything of value.

2. Skills

Knowledge in isolation, without the ability to put it to practical use, is of no value.

Imagine a doctor who has studied the human body in all its intricacies. This person knows all about human anatomy, has learned about the diseases that afflict us, and can discuss any medical problem and its solution. Their knowledge of health and illness is unsurpassed.

Yet this doctor has never once laid hands on a real patient or treated anyone. Their sole source of medical knowledge has come through books they have read, lectures they've attended, and movies they've watched.

Would you want such a person, who has no practical experience treating patients, taking charge of your health? Probably not! This person needs to develop the hands-on skills necessary to practice medicine and treat real patients.

A skill is what a person does with his or her knowledge. It's the learned ability to produce acceptable results with good execution, often within a given amount of time, energy, or both. It's a union of the brain, with its storehouse of knowledge and experience in solving real-world problems, and the body, with its hands and eyes and ears, which acts as the interface between visualization and reality.

Skills come in two general categories.

Hard Skills

Also called technical skills, these relate to a specific occupation, task, or situation. They can be tested, and their use may entail a professional, technical, or academic qualification.

Your "skill set" needs to be in alignment with your occupation. If you're a doctor, you need to know about the various medical devices used in your trade and how to work with them. This comes from having access to such tools and the practical experience of using them. If you happen to have an impressive skill set in some unrelated activity, such as sport fishing, that may be a nice thing for you, but it will not help you become invaluable as a healthcare provider.

The acquisition of hard skills is often dependent on access to the proper physical tools you need to complete a task. Imagine owning a cookbook but lacking a stove or any kitchen tools with which to prepare food. The knowledge might be there in the cookbook, but you need the stove, the mixing bowl, the pots and pans, the utensils, and all the other tools you need to prepare food. You also need the food itself!

If you want to become an invaluable software engineer, you need to know programming languages including Python, Java, C/C++, Scala, and Ruby, as well as other programming fundamentals such as data structures and algorithms; software testing and debugging; object-oriented design (OOD) and its key principles including abstraction, encapsulation, inheritance, decomposition, and generalization; and the fundamentals of software development. While you can teach yourself many of these skills, most people go to school to learn them. And you also need the reference books, thc hardware—the computers that house the software—to exercise your acquired knowledge and skills and to learn new ones.

Overall, to acquire the hard skills you need to become invaluable in your occupation, you need access to the required training, the tools of the trade, and the opportunity to practice your skills in a safe setting.

Soft Skills

These are qualities possessed by most humans to some degree and can be either innate or learned in school. They include personal leadership, problem solving, teamwork, your work ethic, career management, critical thinking, digital literacy, intercultural fluency, having a professional attitude, public speaking, selling, and more. Unlike hard skills, they are not identified with a particular profession, although one profession might require a different mix of soft skills than another.

Soft skills are often called "non-cognitive" skills, which means they cannot be predicted by IQ or achievement tests. While humans have the highest level of soft skills, advanced animals have them too—as the behavior of your pet dog or cat will attest, they're often very good at "reading" what their human roommates want and feel.

As you may be thinking, soft skills are closely related to implicit knowledge, in the sense that they represent the teachable aspects of a body of knowledge, such as the basics of how to do business in China. Soft skills also include tacit knowledge, which is learned only through personal experience, such as the finer points of how to do business in China. For example, anyone can learn the basic soft skills about how to do business in China by reading books or watching YouTube videos. These sources can teach you how to address your Chinese business counterpart, how to pass out business cards, and how to make small talk. This is implicit knowledge that is teachable. The far deeper tacit knowledge you need to learn on your own, or you must have a personal mentor impart his or her knowledge to you. For example, you may know from personal experience that your Chinese counterpart has relatives living in the United

States, and therefore to inquire about their health would be a helpful gesture of empathy.

Soft skills can be acquired or learned at any time and any stage in life. In 1986, author Robert Fulghum published his book, *All I Really Need to Know I Learned in Kindergarten: Uncommon Thoughts on Common Things*, which became a bestseller. Among the precepts Fulghum learned in kindergarten were:

Share everything.

Play fair.

Don't hit people.

Put things back where you found them.

Clean up your own mess.

And many more...[8]

These are skills that make it possible for humans to work together in teams. If you're a hermit living in a cabin deep in a remote forest, you probably don't need soft skills because you're not interacting with other people. But if you're like most of the seven billion human inhabitants of our planet, you're regularly involved in team efforts, whether that's at work, at home, or in the town square.

To get anything done with other people—not to mention to become invaluable—the first soft skill you need is language. You need to be able to communicate with the people around you! What changed the course of the world and the leading role of *Homo sapiens* is when common language was developed. This enabled humans, specifically *Homo sapiens,* to catapult to the top of the world's food chain. They could now plan and adjust to outsmart all other animal species. You need a common set of rules that govern behavior, especially when you're

8 Robert Fulghum. https://www.amazon.com/Really-Need-Know-Learned-Kindergarten/dp/0345466179/ref=tmm_hrd_swatch_0?_encoding=UTF8&qid=&sr=

engaged in any exchange of value, like buying something or getting paid. You need to know how to read other people and have empathy for them, and—especially if you want to be invaluable—you have to be able to reach their hearts and convince them to take a certain course of action or adopt a certain belief, like a politician or other leader can.

How you can "win friends and influence people" (to borrow a phrase from Dale Carnegie) depends quite a bit on your own personality type and your ability to recognize it and use it properly. For thousands of years, philosophers and then scientists have classified human personality types using four broad categories. They began with earth, air, fire, and water, as described by Empodocles in 444 BCE. In the Socratic era, these four quadrants evolved from external environmental factors to internal factors, prompting Hippocrates to redefine them as choleric, sanguine, phlegmatic, and melancholic. Relating them to body chemistry, he called them the four temperaments, and this analysis was accepted well into the early 20th century.

In his 1913 masterpiece, *Psychological Types*, Carl Jung attributed the difference in personality styles not to body chemistry but to the way the brain thinks and processes information. He proposed four basic functions: thinking (T), feeling (F), sensing / sensation (S) and intuition (N).

He believed that emotion-based thinking cannot be properly described as thinking at all, since it "doesn't follow its own logical principle but is subordinated to the principle of feeling."

In 1928, William Moulton Marston built on Jung's work by introducing the four-quadrant behavior model in his book *Emotions of Normal People*. Marston described behavior as occurring along two axes (active vs. passive and favorable vs. antagonistic). By placing the axes at right angles, four quadrants were created with each quadrant describing a behavioral pattern.[9]

Marston defined the four quadrants of personality as Dominance, Influence, Steadiness, and Compliance. This led to the DiSC Assessment, developed in 1940 by Walter Clark, which is used today in DISC Personality Tests.

How does this relate to soft skills? Because if you know your own personality type and that of someone you are speaking with or coaching, you can more effectively reach them. Let's say you're in a discussion with a high D personality. Daniel has plenty of critical thinking, sense-making, and resilience but is weak in empathy. His communication style is sharp and brusque, which has caused issues in working across the organization. You can review with Daniel the importance of empathizing with other employees and being more relaxed in his conversations. Linking simple changes in how he operates leads to better results and can be key to Daniel altering his behavior so that people will be more receptive to him. He could do this through adjusting non-verbal communication, more empathetic ways of writing emails, and even making casual chitchat a habit before getting down to business.

Human resources experts are increasingly focused on the importance of soft skills for labor market success. The evidence is overwhelming that these skills are important drivers of success in school and in adult life. In job listings, in addition to the ubiquitous education and experience qualifications, employers frequently list teamwork, collaboration, and communication skills as highly valuable qualities in potential new hires. A 2017 survey by the National Association of Colleges and Employers

9 Lukas, J. F. & Lukas, J. A. (2009). Pardon me—your personality is showing! Paper presented at PMI® Global Congress 2009—North America, Orlando, FL. Newtown Square, PA: Project Management Institute.

found that "problem-solving skills and an ability to work in a team" were the most commonly desired attributes of new college graduates for employers looking to hire. Other soft skills employers wanted were written communication skills, leadership, and a strong work ethic.[10]

Look at it this way. An employer can easily send you to school to learn additional knowledge or a hard skill. Companies do this all the time—they send their employees to earn advanced degrees or get certified in a technical field. Teaching a person, sharing additional knowledge, and a new job skill is a relatively straightforward process.

It's also possible to teach some soft skills that are common to any business or community role. Courses on public speaking and leadership abound, and consultants reap fortunes advising leaders and managers how to more effectively communicate with their stakeholders. Companies that do business in foreign countries, and in particular the Pacific Rim and the Middle East, have executives who must meet with their foreign counterparts in their native land. These executives often require training in the local language and customs and need to learn how to interact with their foreign counterparts. The goal is to develop mutual trust so that deals can be made to make both sides invaluable to each other.

But there is no seminar or training program that can make a dishonest person become honest, help someone overcome deep-rooted biases, or turn an aggressive control freak into someone who wants to form an equitable partnership with another. These are fundamental personality traits that by the time a person is an adult are fully formed and cannot be improved without intensive therapy, into which no company will invest.

---

10 NACE. https://www.naceweb.org/about-us/press/2017/the-key-attributes-employers-seek-on-students-resumes/

While it's difficult to change someone's personality traits, skills can be adaptable. In fact, adaptability is one of the most useful and often-employed soft skills. People who are adaptable have the flexibility to react to feedback from their boss, change with changing industries, and work well in teams. Some examples of adaptability include:

- **Having a backup plan.** You may have a vision about the way something is going to go, such as your presentation to a group, but sometimes circumstances change and you need to pivot. Is your skill set ready to improvise a new solution?

- **Meeting a changing schedule.** You may have your day planned down to the minute, and suddenly your boss makes a change in a meeting time or your partner calls and says you need to come home to help with a family crisis. A rigid personality will resent such challenges, while an adaptable personality will go with the flow.

- **Embracing new technologies.** Technology can be challenging, and often we take the time and energy to master a new technology, only to have it vanish and be replaced! The rate of change is getting faster, and our collective learning curve is getting steeper. If you want to be invaluable, this may be part of your world. And if you have trouble with a new digital technology, get advice from any fifth-grader, and he or she will enlighten you. (Just kidding.)

- **Being a team player.** Especially if you are a "driver" type personality, being on a team with people of various abilities and viewpoints can be frustrating because to you the answer may be clear—but you're not the boss, and your teammates may have other ideas. This may mean compromising with your team members to come to agreements and making changes when your team members want you to.

- **Coping with disappointment.** This can be very difficult for success-oriented people. But setbacks are a part of life, and we all need to be able to handle them with grace and resilience. Every defeat is an opportunity to learn, and it's only by making mistakes—and being momentarily weak—are we able to become stronger.

Being adaptable is a critical part of having a positive attitude, which we'll discuss next.

3. Attitude

Attitude is what a person *feels* about his or her knowledge and skills reflected in their behavior. It's all about whether a person wants to leverage these attributes to become invaluable or take them for granted and, for whatever reason, fail to exploit them.

There are plenty of people who have knowledge about a particular subject and the skills to accomplish something. Some people are grateful for this and are eager to put these assets to good use. They see them as a bridge to becoming invaluable.

While you would think success and invaluableness would come easily to people with knowledge and skills, often the opposite is true, and these qualified people just drift along with the current. They never reach their full potential and even try to *avoid* becoming invaluable.

You often see this in sports. Before the big game, the coach will try to inspire the team to win. The coach knows that according to the statistics her team has every chance to beat their opponent. But there's one big problem: the players have no will to win. They don't have that "fire in the belly" that is the hallmark of a champion. The coach can try to instill this winning spirit in her players—that's one of the most important parts of a coach's job, whether in sports or in a corporation—but it can be difficult because a winning attitude is often something a person has developed within themselves...or they haven't. If not, it takes a very concerted effort by the individual to develop such an attitude or level of self-worth to go beyond what others are capable of achieving. In *Becoming Invaluable*, we will spell out the difference makers, but only you can implement them in your life to a level beyond what others will consider through commitment, discipline, and resolve to continuously develop yourself.

One of the key strategies for developing a winning attitude is to change the expectations of the person from *expecting to lose* to *working to win*. For example, one of the biggest challenges facing military recruiters is that they're obliged to enlist all sorts of people who walk through the door, and many of these people are looking for a paying job in uniform because they have nowhere else to go. Many have knowledge and can be taught skills, but they have poor attitudes and see themselves as screw-ups—far from invaluable! Talent and skill are two different things, talent is what God gives us and skill is the discipline applied to create excellence. Military leaders use all sorts of techniques to forge motley groups of individuals into winning teams, such as making everyone wear the same uniform and live by the same rules. One of the simplest techniques is this. *Every morning, you make your bed according to specifications*. It sounds almost silly, but it's important that every recruit succeeds at this simple task.

Here's what made it famous. On May 17, 2014, Admiral William H. McRaven addressed the graduating class of the University of Texas at Austin on their commencement day. He shared the ten principles he learned during Navy SEAL training that helped him overcome challenges both in his long career and throughout his life. One of them was "Make your bed," and it became so well known that he wrote a bestselling book, *Make Your Bed: Little Things That Can Change Your Life...And Maybe the World*.

As he explained, "You roll out of bed, and you just make your bed, you make it straight. Again, you get it right too. It's not just about kind of throwing the covers over the pillow. It's about making your bed right and walking away and going, 'OK, that's good. That looks good. As simple as it sounds, I'm proud of this little task I did.' And that is really what I think sets the tone for the rest of the day. It is the simplicity. I think it is also the amount of time that it takes to make your bed. It doesn't take an hour to do, and yet you get this sense of accomplishment."[11]

It's a small thing, but big change is made only with small steps that are successfully completed. For some recruits, making their bed in the morning is a new idea. But it's simple enough that anyone can master it. And what's more, there is often a limit on how much time you have to get it done. And guess what? It's very difficult to do it right all by yourself in the allotted time. Recruits quickly learn that if they *help each other make their beds* they can all get the job done in time. They learn to do a simple task using teamwork, and that leaves an impression in their minds.

If you are not a member of the military, you need to develop the attitude through your own development of knowledge and skills in order to help yourself know you can achieve invaluableness. It's real work over time to truly reach invaluableness.

Amazingly, in some scenarios, you can achieve temporary and perhaps unethical success with exceptional soft skills, very little knowledge or hard skills, and a relentless attitude. We're talking about some politicians and other job seekers who are able to use their power of persuasion—a super soft skill—to convince people to vote for them or hire them, even though they have none of the job qualifications for the position they seek. They present themselves as invaluable and have the communication skills to pull it off, but when they actually get the

---

11 BusinessInsider. https://www.businessinsider.com/navy-seal-commander-explains-why-you-should-make-your-bed-2017-4

job it's revealed they have little grasp of the realities of what they need to do. Such people are usually exposed and wind up being shown the door.

A key aspect of attitude is your willingness to adapt to the situation you're in and the people around you at any given moment, thereby allowing you to become more invaluable. An obvious and simple example would be the language you speak. For example, our nation is becoming increasingly multicultural. Data from the U.S. Department of Labor indicates that by the year 2030, nearly forty million people of Hispanic origin will be in the nation's workforce. In the decade until 2030, Hispanics are projected to account for seventy-eight percent of net new workers.[12] Because they're new workers, they're likely to be front-line employees in agriculture, restaurants, hotels, manufacturing, healthcare, and transportation.

The question is this. If you're a manager and speak only English, you may find yourself at a disadvantage. Sure, you can say, "All my employees need to speak English! It's not my job to learn their language!" You can *say* that, but it will mean that you'll forfeit a degree of influence with them. By adapting and learning some basic Spanish phrases that are used on the job, you'll become more invaluable to your employees.

As the famous Speaker of the U.S. House of Representatives Sam Rayburn said, "If you want to get along, go along." By the way, the colorful Texan also said, "You can't be a leader and ask other people to follow you unless you know how to follow too." You cannot be invaluable to others until you let them know they're valuable to you, too.

Meet people halfway. And if you show an interest in learning their language, they'll be more inclined to learn yours.

---

12 USDOL. https://blog.dol.gov/2021/09/15/hispanics-in-the-labor-force-5-facts

The Four Styles of Communication

Swiss psychologist Carl Jung proposed four styles of human communication. These styles are based on tendencies to be take-charge vs. easygoing and task-oriented vs. people-oriented. While these are simplifications, tendencies of the four styles are:

1. **Controllers.** They take charge and want control of themselves, others, and situations. Task-oriented drivers are only focused on the end goal. They often express a sense of urgency with louder volume and express limited to no emotion.

When communicating with a controller, communicate confidently with a clear and concise message. Don't mince words. Ask straightforward questions. State what's in it for them. Avoid needless clutter and fluff.

2. **Collaborators.** Easygoing, relationship-oriented, and enjoy working with people to work toward a consensus, they appear relaxed but highly emotional with an expressive tone, ask many questions, have a win-win attitude, and are hesitant to make unilateral decisions.

When communicating with a collaborator, show an interest in what they have to say. Listen patiently and find common ground in your message or what you're asking them to do.

3. **Analyzers.** These are detail-oriented, logical thinkers who analyze others and situations. Work best alone to come up with solutions and therefore may take more time to make a decision and take action. In their demeanor, they are cautious, logical thinkers with a soft-spoken, monotone voice, using limited eye contact and facial expressions.

When communicating with an analyzer, avoid needless chitchat, quietly present just the facts, data, and pertinent details, and explain the process you'll follow to service them.

4. Socializers. They are outgoing, enjoy meeting people, and thrive on change. They get their energy from others and work best when brainstorming with others to make a decision and take action. Outspoken, quick to make a decision, and assertive, these fast talkers express how they're feeling through gestures, facial expressions, and tone.

When communicating with a socializer, show a personal interest in them. Be upbeat, find a common experience, and relate their personal experiences to your message. Be responsive!

Other psychologists and experts have proposed their own categories, so if you do more research, don't be surprised to find these types and more:

Director, relator, analyzer, socializer—Dr. Tony Alessandra.

Listener, creator, doer, thinker—Dr. Paul Mot.

Intuitor, thinker, feeler, senser—iSpeak Interaction Styles.

Director, expressor, thinker, harmonizer—Eric Douglas.

But they all go back to Carl Jung!

By being aware of the communication preferences of yourself and others, you'll have a better understanding of how others perceive you and of how you can reach them. The ability to recognize and adapt to your listeners' communication styles will make them feel like you've cared enough to listen and focus on their needs. This strengthens the relationship and results in a positive experience.

Ask yourself: What does your communication style communicate to others? Does a lack of eye contact communicate you're disinterested? Does your distracted expression communicate you don't want to be there? Or does your direct stare suggest aggressiveness? Does your loud speech tell them you're trying to steamroll them into agreeing with you?

Use the strategy of *mirroring*, where you reproduce the other person's verbal and nonverbal communication cues in order to make them feel comfortable. This may sound cynical and manipulative, but it's really an exercise in humility where you get in sync with the other person's style in an effort to eliminate cultural or personality gaps. For example, when you meet a Chinese businessperson, you'll probably shake hands, bow, and perhaps even applaud each other before exchanging business cards. By going along with this ritual, you show respect and put your counterpart at ease.

The Four Steps to Adapting

No matter which communication style you use, you can take certain steps to open the doors to finding a solution to a problem. If you take these four steps in order, you'll make the connection with the person or situation that will strengthen the bond between you and help make you more invaluable.

1) Identify the Need

Before you try to adapt to any situation or group, you first need to pinpoint what's keeping you apart. What's preventing you from making a connection or the other party from seeing you as invaluable? It could be a language barrier. It could be a variation in personal viewpoints, differing business strategies, or gaps in technical training. It could be a difference in communication styles even if you speak the same language.

The key here is to be honest with yourself. Our initial impulse might be to see the gap or variation as being the other guy's responsibility. For example, with the language barrier, a boss might say, "It's not my job to learn the language of immigrant workers. It's their responsibility to learn ours." Really? Is that how you make yourself invaluable to them?

By the way, it would be a good idea to make clear that in your drive to become invaluable, we *don't mean invaluable only to those who are above you on the ladder*. Trying to become invaluable only to your superior and not to anyone else is basically the definition of "sucking up to the boss." That's not what this is about. True leaders are what we call "Invaluable 360." That means you're invaluable to everyone around you—your boss, your colleagues, your subordinates, your customers, your family, and your community. It means that you're giving more than you're taking. Not that you should exhaust yourself or sacrifice your own mental and physical health, but rather you're using an approach that's measured and confident.

Back to being honest with yourself, if you look at the language barrier objectively, wouldn't it make sense for both parties to try to learn each other's language? If you've ever gone to a foreign country with some knowledge of the local tongue, and the person you're talking to has some grasp of English, it's fun to communicate using a mashup of both languages—a little English here, a little Spanish there.

Adapting may mean going back to school and learning a new skill. It may mean embracing new federal or state workplace regulations. It may mean making adjustments to your own schedule as you have a family or near retirement age.

2) Adapt Your Mindset

By identifying the problem, you've taken the first step toward removing barriers. But it's quite possible to correctly recognize the problem (we have a language barrier), pinpoint the solution (I should learn some Spanish!), and then fail to take action—especially when the solution requires you to make a change within yourself (I have no time, it takes too long, the company won't pay for it).

You need to develop the mental space necessary to adjust your mindset in alignment with evolving circumstances. Put aside your preconceived ideas and be ready for the new dynamic.

A root of inflexibility can be an exaggerated belief that life in the past was better than it is today. To many people, change can be threatening. They have a rosy view of yesterday and a darker view of today and tomorrow, usually due to circumstances they believe are beyond their control. They think new technologies are threatening, workplace human resources rules are frustrating, and culture shifts are bewildering.

How can you change your mindset so that you can move forward with the solution that you've recognized as being important? Take it step by step. Old attitudes are hard to break. The best way to let go of old negative attitudes is to focus on helping other people. Ask yourself, "How can I make their life better? Oh—there is a way. I'll give it a shot."

3) Set the Goal

In any endeavor, it's important to define the goal. This makes planning possible and allows you to allocate time and resources without either wasting them or falling short. It also gives everyone involved a feeling of satisfaction when the goal is reached. Goals can be very simple. Remember what Admiral William H. McRaven said about making your bed every morning. It's a simple task and a simple goal, but it contributes to a feeling of self-esteem and of being valuable.

For example, if the problem is that you and your team members have a language barrier, and you've accepted the fact that it would be helpful if you learned some Spanish, then you should set your initial goal at learning basic conversational phrases that apply to the workplace. You probably will never have to learn how to say, "Let's go dancing tonight," because you're working, but you'll certainly want to say, "Here's your paycheck," (which happens to be, "*Aquí está su cheque de pago.*")

4) Implement the Plan

This is where the rubber meets the road, so to speak. You can adjust your attitude and see the problem and make a plan, but the only way to have an effect and make yourself invaluable is to take action.

You do that by giving yourself mini-goals that you will accomplish *right now*. If you're learning a foreign language to make yourself invaluable at work, then sit down right now and order one of those language learning courses. Or call in an employee who's bilingual and offer to hire them to teach you. When you drive to work, play the foreign language in your car. Subscribe to a foreign language newspaper. Force yourself to learn some new words every day.

The key to long-term success and to becoming invaluable is to possess and ethically employ the three attributes of knowledge, skills, attitude. You need all three, and you can learn all three if you have an open mind and truly want to be a leader in your community. In developing your knowledge, skills, and attitude, you are further enabling willitude and navigotiation by having a real compass in life. This compass develops from having a strong purpose and a clear set of values both of which support your vision and mission (goals and objectives). All aspects support you in achieving your chosen outcomes and enable you to help turn any weaknesses or barriers into additional strength as you strive toward your desired outcome.

Invaluable Spotlight Profile: Jim Gans

Jim Gans is the president of Image Marketing Enterprises LLC, a franchise company that enables students to learn the most effective methods of presenting themselves in the entertainment business or in any business environment.

Jim learned from his dad that you need to be focused and shouldn't always look for the next best thing—concentrate on what's happening today.

When the Covid-19 pandemic hit, he had to keep the business running, so he put together a "Team of the Best" with his best techs, sales team, content team, logistics people, and customer care teams, and had them brainstorm for seven days without speaking to each other on how they could run the company virtually. In four weeks, their technology people built a system, and they eventually enrolled three thousand paying students into the online program.

Failure was not an option. He had to succeed for his family.

Jim says you must care about the people who work with you. "With" is the key word, because people work *with* Jim, not for him. Loyalty is a two-way street.

If asked what he fears the most in life, Jim is likely to reply, "It's being poor." He says that for his entire life, he knew he didn't want to be poor. He saw too many of his father's friends who did well for themselves end up having nothing left later in life to retire with.

To be invaluable means to be loyal and have commitment.

4. Health

We all live in the physical world. We enter it as helpless babies. We grow up, become adults, and hopefully live long and productive lives. Then we grow old and die. This is the way of the world, and whether you're a pauper or a billionaire, that's the cycle. No one is an exception.

But we know that between the boundaries of birth and death, there can be extreme variations. Some babies perish before they leave the crib. Others are born with afflictions that impede their full growth and potential, and yet they live long lives. Some of us survive and thrive for a century or more—as of this writing, the oldest known person on earth, a French nun, has just passed away at the age of one hundred and eighteen.

In general—because there are exceptions—enjoying good health is one key to becoming invaluable, simply because if you're in good health you're not impeded by bad health. Chronic disease drains time and resources from you and is a psychological burden. Healthcare is expensive, especially in the United States; in 2021, our health care spending reached $4.3 trillion, or $12,914 per person. The average includes all the healthy people who spent very little—roughly twenty percent of the population consumes eighty percent of our healthcare costs.

With infectious diseases becoming more infrequent than in the past, we're now grappling with a rising tide of chronic "lifestyle" diseases such as heart disease, diabetes, and obesity. According to the Centers for Disease Control and Prevention (CDC), more than thirty-seven million Americans have diabetes, and another ninety-six million have prediabetes, which puts them at risk for type 2 diabetes. The disease, which is linked to obesity and insulin resistance, can cause other conditions including heart disease, kidney failure, and blindness. In 2017, the total estimated cost of diagnosed diabetes was $327 billion in medical costs and lost productivity.

Obesity affects twenty percent of children and forty-two percent of adults, putting them at risk of chronic diseases such as type 2 diabetes, heart disease, and some cancers. It costs the US health care system nearly $173 billion a year, and over twenty-five percent of young people aged seventeen to twenty-four are too heavy to join the US military.[13]

Some aspects of our health are beyond our control. We inherit our genes from our parents. No one is born perfect—we all have some sort of physical shortcoming. We live in areas that may be polluted or have poor access to healthy food. Childhood trauma or abuse can affect how we view ourselves and our bodies.

But despite our defects, we have significant control over our health. We can learn to eat properly, get our vaccinations, live in a clean environment, and get enough exercise. Health and attitude tend to go hand in hand. The healthier you are, the happier and more positive you tend to be. Of course there are amazing exceptions—one need only think of Stephen Hawking, who at age twenty-one was diagnosed with an early-onset slow-progressing form of motor neuron disease that gradually, over decades, paralyzed him. Confined to a wheelchair and deprived of the power of speech, he cheerfully soldiered on, and until his death at the age of seventy-nine he served as one of the world's most celebrated scientists.

13 CDC. https://www.cdc.gov/chronicdisease/about/costs/index.htm

The bottom line is this. If nature provided you with a functioning, healthy body, then you owe it to yourself to take good care of it. Here are some important exercises and tips to help you reach your peak mental and physical wellbeing. After all, you only get one body, and there are no refunds!

Mental Health

The body and the mind should work with perfect synergy, and what affects one will impact the other. A poor diet and lack of physical conditioning can have a negative effect on your thinking and your attitude, while depression or a poor mental state can make you more susceptible to disease, and if you get sick you may take longer to heal.

To become invaluable and to be able to offer a robust amount of knowledge and skills with a positive attitude, you need to have a strong mind. While the vast universe of human psychology is far beyond the scope of this book, we can offer key insights on the importance of mental health in business.

For example, employee burnout is increasing. According to the World Health Organization, workplace burnout is driven by a chronic imbalance between job demands and job resources—that is to say, what your boss wants and what you can deliver. Correlated with anxiety and depression, it's characterized by extreme tiredness, reduced ability to regulate cognitive and emotional processes, and mental distancing.

What can you do to maintain peak mental health so that you can become and remain invaluable? Here are the top five things you can do to stay sharp.

1. Get enough sleep. This is at the top of the list for a reason! We live in a culture where many of us are chronically sleep deprived, either because of unavoidable circumstance (such as a new baby in the house) or by our choice. Sleep deprivation erodes peak performance. Without proper sleep, you stumble through the day feeling scatterbrained, foggy, and unfocused. You depend on the caffeine in your coffee to get a charge on your brain, which locks you into a cycle of sleepiness and more caffeine. Serious sleep deprivation can lead to depression, severe mood swings, the danger of falling asleep at the wheel, and even hallucinations.

Most adults need seven to eight hours sleep each night. Contrary to what many so-called "hard chargers" will tell you, sleep is *not* just wasted time. While you're asleep, your brain is busy processing what it learned during the day and preparing for tomorrow. Research suggests that sleep plays a housekeeping role, removing toxins in your brain that build up while you're awake. Sleeping helps strengthen memories you've formed throughout the day while linking new memories to earlier ones—and often coming up with innovative ideas.

You can get enough sleep if you make it a priority.

- Set a schedule. Go to bed and wake up at the same time each day.

- Before going to bed, turn off your electronics! Your bed is the place for just two activities: sleep and sex. Do not bring your phone or pad to bed. You can live without them for seven hours.

- Exercise every day, but not just before you go to bed. It is best to exercise early in the day to charge your body and brain through the natural body processes that are a direct benefit of exercise.

- Avoid caffeine and nicotine late in the day. Let those powerful stimulants wear off before you retire for the night.

- If you cannot sleep, don't just toss and turn. Do something else, like read a real book or listen to music, until you feel tired. Do not stare at a screen.

If you sleep *too much*—like more than nine hours a day—and you're still sleepy during the day, then you may have hypersomnia, a medical condition. See your doctor!

To be invaluable, you need to be mentally sharp. Get there and stay there by getting the right amount of sleep.

2. Keep learning. Research—and common sense—say that the human brain stays healthy and fit with continued learning. Your brain is like a muscle—the more you use it, the stronger it gets. When you learn something, new neural connections are created, which improves your capacity to think creatively.

In addition to experiencing the pleasure of continued learning, people who engage in mentally stimulating activities reduce their risk for cognitive decline. This does not need to be formal instruction in school; participating in social events, playing an instrument, reading, dancing, creating art, playing board games, and doing other activities that require mental and social engagement stimulate cognitive fitness.

To get the maximum benefit from a brain training exercise, don't just do the same thing over and over again. Your brain needs to be challenged with new forms of stimulation. Try something you haven't done before, such as doing math in your head, reading a new book, or learning a foreign language. The Global Council on Brain Health (GCBH) calls these "cognitively stimulating activities," or CSAs. At any age, engaging in CSAs can help your brain generate new neurons and create new neuron connections. This impacts memory, attention, thinking, language, and reasoning skills.

One more note. In recent years we've seen an explosion in the number of "brain pills" being marketed to adults and senior citizens. These pills claim to support brain health, improve your memory, make you mentally sharper, and so forth. Think carefully before you spend your money on these products! Most of them contain ordinary vitamins and minerals that you can—and should—get with a healthy diet and a daily multivitamin. One such brain pill says that its secret ingredient is a protein found in jellyfish, which makes it special.

Jellyfish? Really? The scientific fact is that your proteins are made by your body for yourself, and your protein molecules are genetically individual to you alone. When you consume protein—whether from a juicy steak, a piece of tofu, or a jellyfish—your body immediately breaks it down into its component amino acids. There are just twenty amino acids that your body uses to build the thousands of different proteins it needs. You need to know that *your body does not care where these amino acids come from.* Cow, soybean, chicken, tuna, jellyfish—all of these are nothing more than sources of these ubiquitous building blocks from which your body makes its own proteins. If you want to pay a premium price for jellyfish protein, go ahead, but your body will tear it apart just like any other.

Is there a powerful placebo effect with these brain pills? Yes, there is. People who take a brain pill with the belief that it will improve their brain function may experience improvement simply because they *believe* they will. The brain has tremendous powers of self-persuasion!

Among other things, being invaluable means having specialized knowledge others don't have but want. Life is change, and you should keep one step ahead by steadily learning new things!

3. Keep laughing. Yes, literally laughing; but more broadly speaking, try to find the fun and humor in life. You'll live longer, and studies even show that a good sense of humor and high intelligence often go hand in hand.

Researchers in Austria discovered that funny people have higher IQs than their dour peers. They believe it takes both cognitive and emotional ability to process and produce humor. Funny people, it seems, have higher verbal and nonverbal intelligence, and they score lower in mood disturbance and aggressiveness.[14] Additionally, here's an observation from Steve's experiences. Two people, one a close friend and the other a work friend of his friend, were two of the most invaluable programmers working in this relatively stodgy financial institution. They are two of the funniest people Steve has ever met in life. It carried over into their work in unique ways. They even took an empty office, put a single chair in the room and a tennis ball, covered the doors and windows, and when stuck on something or needing a break they would individually, or together, go into the room and play a weird game of handball, laughing and carrying on while their brains worked subconsciously on the issue at hand. Even though fellow workers would laugh or scoff at them, they carried on becoming more and more invaluable. Once rejuvenated, energized, and perhaps even with some new ideas, they would go back to work motivated to solving the issues in their programming.

Steve never understood why they had the chair in the room. Perhaps when alone they challenged themselves to throw or hit the ball and make it come back from various angles. Fun, laughter, movement, and even frustration create and release energy, building mental wellbeing with a sense of joy.

---

14 Newsweek. https://www.newsweek.com/funny-people-higher-iq-more-intelligent-685585

For a study in Turkey, more than two hundred children were asked to write captions for ten cartoon images. Seven adults then rated the humor of the captions and their relevance to the cartoons with a total of 30,380 ratings. Then the intelligence and cartoon caption humor performance of these children were compared, and the researchers found that general intelligence was highly correlated with how the cartoons had been ranked for their humor. Children with higher general knowledge and higher verbal reasoning were found to have higher humor ability.[15]

Humor can be a form of tacit knowledge and is shaped by cultural norms, beliefs, and values. The influence of intelligence on humorous behaviors should be evaluated in the context of specific cultures. A joke considered hilarious in one culture may not be funny in another. A particular behavior may be considered a sign of high intelligence in one culture, but another may find such behavior inappropriate.

People are drawn to other people who have a lively sense of humor. In your journey to becoming invaluable, you can be sure that being able to make yourself and others laugh will help you get there.

4. Pursue your purpose. Uniquely among all the animals on earth, humans are capable of recognizing their current state, sensing their own dissatisfaction with it, imagining a better future state, and taking action to achieve it. This is all thanks to our superior brain, that three-pound lump of fat, protein, and water, which is the most complex object in the known universe. (Think about that for a minute. It's true. As far as we know, your brain is the most sophisticated thing anywhere of any size.) You can call this your purpose, your goal, your

---

15 Phys.org. https://phys.org/news/2021-10-ability-humor-linked-higher-intelligence.html

dream—by any name, it means to make life better for yourself or others.

A sense of purpose in life is the extent to which someone feels that their life has direction and has ultimate goals. Among different people, a strong sense of purpose looks different. Everyone is entitled to their own definition. Some people may want to be successful in their career, some to contribute to their community, and some to take care of their families or others.

This was the focus of a study led by Dr. Koichiro Shiba, assistant professor at Boston University's School of Public Health in Massachusetts. According to the results, having a purpose lowers the risk of all causes of mortality, regardless of gender, race, or ethnicity. The effects were more pronounced among women. The study, "Purpose in life and eight-year mortality by gender and race/ethnicity among older adults in the U.S," analyzed a diverse, large, and nationwide sample of older adults in the United States, looking for relationships between a sense of purpose and mortality across gender, race, and ethnicity.

The analysis of roughly ten thousand people revealed that those with the strongest sense of purpose lowered their risk of death by 15.2% compared to people with the least sense of purpose. Results showed that the highest levels of purpose appeared to be protective against all causes of mortality regardless of socio-economic status.[16]

In its simplest form, you can spotlight your purpose by asking yourself this question: "Why do I exist?"

Your answer might be, "To help other people lead better lives," or "To increase human knowledge of the world," or "To feed people."

16 Koichiro Shiba, Laura D. Kubzansky, David R. Williams, Tyler J. VanderWeele, Eric S. Kim, Purpose in life and 8-year mortality by gender and race/ethnicity among older adults in the U.S, Preventive Medicine, Volume 164, 2022, 107310, ISSN 0091-7435, https://doi.org/10.1016/j.ypmed.2022.107310.

If those seem too broad, you might make it more specific to your vocation, such as, "I want to be a successful pianist and bring music to millions," or "I want to help prevent and solve crimes, thereby keeping people safe."

It's always better to state your purpose in terms of how you will help other people. After all, if you're not helping other people to lead better lives, you're not exactly invaluable, are you? In fact, if people don't need you because you're acting purely for yourself, then you're disposable. No one wants that! By focusing on helping other people, you set up a better way to judge your success in becoming invaluable.

For example, Steve's purpose in life is to support and care for his family in the best possible way financially while being a husband and father with high values and standards. This purpose continues to carry Steve beyond the various roles of building and selling his company to today teaching his family how to manage the financial position they have achieved for generations to come and imparting his learned experience to his children and grandchildren.

Purpose is the driving force creating passion, perseverance, and motivation that impacts everything in life including personal, relational, and occupational pursuits. Understanding this simple but profound concept captures not just the imagination but the driving force to accomplish goals and aspirations on all fronts of life.

Terry's purpose has remained the same for a few decades: to live daily to impact and influence everyone possible. This simple but profound mindset has allowed him to touch lives all over the world by sharing his story of personal brokenness. He's been able to relate to those who are also broken and who need healing through purpose alignment, which extends beyond who we are to who we can be with guided direction and the intention to succeed. More on establishing your purpose in life just ahead.

5. Stay connected to other people. From the day you were born, social interaction has been a major part of your cognitive development. Early relationships and interactions with parents, siblings, friends, and teachers taught you how to speak, interpret and express emotions, and expand your knowledge of the world around you.

As an adult, socialization remains key to brain health. A good way to keep your mind agile and improve cognitive function is to build social networks and participate in social activities. These are like exercises for your brain because they can help prevent mental decline and lower the risk of dementia.

Close and supportive relationships with family and friends can decrease depression and anxiety, facilitating better cognitive function. When you have people to lean on for emotional support, you'll have clearer, faster brain function.

In a 2008 study by Harvard School of Public Health (HSPH), researchers tested a large group of Americans age fifty and older over a period of six years. They read each person a list of ten common nouns then asked them to recall as many words as possible immediately and after a five-minute delay. Their level of social integration was assessed by marital status, volunteer activities, and contact with parents, children, and neighbors. The results showed that individuals with the highest social integration had the slowest rate of memory decline. In fact, memory decline among the most integrated was less than half the rate among the least integrated.[17]

17 "Effects of Social Integration on Preserving Memory Function in a Nationally Representative U.S. Elderly Population," Karen A. Ertel, M. Maria Glymour, Lisa F. Berkman, American Journal of Public Health, July 2008, Vol. 98, No. 7.

By definition, being invaluable means being active within a group of other people—at work, in the community, at home, at church. The fact that you are engaged is one of the elements that will help keep you mentally sharp—which helps you to stay engaged. It's a virtuous cycle.

Physical Health

Thanks to modern science, we know that mental health, physical health, and your ability to be a fully contributing member of society are inexorably linked. Your brain is supported by your body and vice versa. Good health allows you to do God's good work here on earth.

For several key reasons, becoming invaluable and being in the best possible health are mutually dependent on each other.

You need to show up. Even though we increasingly rely on video conferencing, thus lessening the need to travel, the best leaders appear in person to communicate and plan. There is still no substitute for face-to-face meetings, and the more responsibility you have, the more frequent these meetings will be, and sometimes they'll be quite large. You may be asked to deliver a TED talk or an address at a big convention or seminar. You may have hundreds or even thousands of people watching you and listening to you. Think about politicians who need to debate on national television, professional athletes at the big game, or pop musicians playing a concert in a stadium. The day and time are set well in advance, and there are no excuses—they need to be there and ready to perform!

You need to look healthy. Yes, it's true—people judge leaders in part by how they look. Probably the most famous example of this is the first presidential election television debate between Richard Nixon and John F. Kennedy.

On Monday, September 26, 1960, for the first time in American history, a debate between major party presidential candidates was broadcast on television. The day unfolded very differently for the two candidates. Nixon, the presumed front-runner, had pledged to visit all fifty states during his campaign, and was exhausted after traveling and then spending three weeks in the hospital with a badly inflamed knee. On the day of the debate in the studios of WBBM-TV in Chicago, he made several other campaign stops around the city and gave a speech at a Chicago Carpenters Union event. Tired and gaunt, when his car arrived at the TV station, he climbed out of the back seat and bashed his injured knee against the door frame.

Meanwhile, Kennedy, who had spent the week off the campaign trail, preparing for the debate with mock opponents, relaxed, worked on his suntan, and listened to records by 1950s songstress Peggy Lee.

At the studio, Kennedy was offered makeup for the camera, and he refused. Overhearing that, Nixon likewise declined. But Kennedy was tanned and rested, while Nixon was pale and haggard from his hospital stay.

On camera, and sporting his perpetual five o'clock shadow—despite a last-minute application of a beard concealer called LazyShave—Nixon looked tired, hurting, and sweaty. He was also wearing a gray suit, which against the gray background (this was black and white TV) made him appear insubstantial. When Kennedy gave an answer, he looked confidently into the camera, while Nixon addressed the actual reporters on each side of him, giving him a shifty, nervous appearance.

Kennedy, who came in as the underdog against the former vice president, emerged as a credible choice for president, at least among the people who watched the debate on television. But within the smaller audience who tuned in on radio and didn't see the candidates, polls showed that Nixon was still the favorite.

In the second, third, and fourth televised debates, Nixon had learned the hard lessons from the first debate, and he fared better. On election night, the polls showed Kennedy with a slight lead over Nixon---and he narrowly won the presidency.

You need to have stamina. This is generally defined as the energy and strength to continue with a difficult process or effort. There are occasions in life and in business where sheer physical endurance is required to overcome a challenge. While we all agree that getting enough sleep and "down time" is critical for your personal health, there will be times when you need to be on deck, as captain of the ship, for a long period of time. As Greg Brenneman, chairman of CCMP Capital, said, "People want to be led, not managed, in a time of crisis." Crisis time is an optimum opportunity to demonstrate leadership—and you need to be up for the job.

A strategy for maintaining your stamina is to make your work a series of sprints, not a long marathon. Instead of setting long hours each day, look at the times you are most productive, and remove any distractions. Then keep focused and sprint. Go all-out for a few hours, and then stop and take a break. Go outside and take a walk. Clear your head. Brush your teeth. (We're not kidding—when you feel burned out but have morc to do, brushing your teeth can make you feel like a new person.) Stay hydrated. Avoid sugar and fatty foods. Take time to relax and breathe deeply.

Your Good Health Routine

Your health is extremely important, and it cannot happen by accident. You need to work on it, just like you would work on anything else in your life. You need a health routine.

Why have a routine? Like the two funniest people in Steve's life, they developed a routine at work in their special room.

One good reason is that having a daily routine—for all the things you do—reduces your stress levels. Every time you have to make a decision, even a trivial one, you are adding some stress to your life. Creating regular rhythms for all of your daily activities can save you time and increase your efficiency.

Here's an example. When *Vanity Fair* asked President Barack Obama about his daily choices, he replied, "You'll see I wear only gray or blue suits. I'm trying to pare down decisions. I don't want to make decisions about what I'm eating or wearing. Because I have too many other decisions to make."

This is because, he explained, the effort of making one decision erodes your ability to make later decisions. Psychologists call it *decision fatigue*. It's why shopping for groceries can be so exhausting and leaders become less tolerant later in the day.[18]

Your health routine begins when you wake up after getting a good night's sleep. Set your alarm so you have plenty of time to accomplish your morning strength-building routine before you head out the door to work. Don't dither over little things; save your brainpower and focus for big decisions, like whether or not to purchase a home or accept a new job. Always prioritize. You only have a limited amount of time each day, and you can't spend time thinking about everything. Don't get distracted by trivial annoyances. If some fellow commuter cuts you off while you're driving to work, and no harm was done, then forget it. Don't ruminate over it. Get on with what you need to do.

Set aside time for proper meals and exercise. Be religious about this. Even if your family's schedule is busy, create a

---

18 https://www.vanityfair.com/news/2012/10/michael-lewis-profile-barack-obama

weeknight family dinner routine to ensure you and your loved ones have time with each other at the end of the day.

Another reason why it's important to have a set routine is because your body operates on cycles that are deeply embedded, and when you deviate from them, you're not going to feel good. Each one of us has a *circadian rhythm* or cycle, which is a natural, internal process that regulates the sleep–wake cycle and repeats roughly every twenty-four hours. These daily rhythms are driven by your internal circadian clock and include clear patterns of core body temperature, hormone production, brainwave activity, cell regeneration, and other biological activities.

For example, you may be an "early bird" or a "night owl." Left to your own schedule—that is, you can sleep and wake when you want to—your body will naturally settle into its own rhythm. You'll go to sleep and wake up at the same times every day—perhaps even down to the minute. Hopefully, your work schedule corresponds to your circadian rhythm. But if you're a night owl who normally sleeps from midnight to 7:00 AM, you'll have a difficult time if you have to get up at 5:00 every morning to get ready for work. You might think that if you were forced to do this, you'd become sleepy by 10:00 PM, and you would adjust. But that's not what happens. Your circadian rhythm is so deeply embedded that at 10:00 PM, no matter how early you were forced to get up, *you're still wide awake*. You'll stay up until midnight—and then the next morning, you'll drag yourself out of bed after getting only five hours of sleep. You'll be chronically exhausted.

In our culture, it's easier to be an early bird because there's no particular reason why you can't go to bed at ten o'clock. It feels normal to you. Unless, of course, you're a shift worker, defined as someone who works outside of the "normal" hours of 7:00 AM to 6:00 PM. According to the US Bureau of Labor Statistics, approximately sixteen percent of wage and salary employees follow shift work schedules. This includes the six percent who work evening shifts and four percent who work night shifts.[19]

Research studies have documented the physical and mental challenges of shift work. One study found problems ranging from a disruption of biological circadian rhythms and sleep/wake cycle to several psychosomatic troubles and disorders, possibly including cancer, as well as impairment of performance efficiency and family and social life.[20]

Some companies switch workers from day shifts to night shifts and back again. This is incredibly stressful, and unfortunately there's no good answer.

Here's the routine that we recommend for optimizing both your physical and mental health. It's just a suggestion. You can adapt it to suit your lifestyle. The important thing is to make it something you can do every day, or at least a few times per week. Steady repetition is the key to success.

Emotional Health

A person can appear to be in superb physical health and possess all of his or her mental faculties but have significant emotional health issues that can hold them back from not just being invaluable but from effectively functioning at all.

Emotional health can be defined very simply. It's about how you *feel* about yourself and your future. It has nothing to do with what an observer would call your objective reality at the moment. You can be rich or poor, young or old, healthy or sick, famous or obscure, and suffer from emotional pain.

---

19 US BLS. https://www.bls.gov/careeroutlook/2015/article/night-owls-and-early-birds.htm

20 Costa G. Shift work and health: current problems and preventive actions. Saf Health Work. 2010 Dec;1(2):112-23. doi: 10.5491/SHAW.2010.1.2.112. Epub 2010 Dec 30. PMID: 22953171; PMCID: PMC3430894.

In literature, the subject of emotional health was spotlighted brilliantly by Edwin Arlington Robinson in his 1897 poem "Richard Cory."

Whenever Richard Cory went down town,
We people on the pavement looked at him:
He was a gentleman from sole to crown,
Clean favored, and imperially slim.

And he was always quietly arrayed,
And he was always human when he talked;
But still he fluttered pulses when he said,
"Good-morning," and he glittered when he walked.

And he was rich—yes, richer than a king—
And admirably schooled in every grace:
In fine, we thought that he was everything
To make us wish that we were in his place.

So on we worked, and waited for the light,
And went without the meat, and cursed the bread;
And Richard Cory, one calm summer night,
Went home and put a bullet through his head.

We all know people—both celebrities and those in our community—who have taken, or attempted to take, that last final step. A shocking example was the 2018 suicide of Anthony Bourdain, the renowned chef and author who had reached a new level of fame with his television series *Parts Unknown*. In fact, if you're interested in how food shapes your culture, no matter where on earth you live, Bourdain's show was truly invaluable. There was simply no other program like it. And yet, despite his wealth and the fact that he was providing a real service to his fellow humans, which you'd think would have brought him great satisfaction, Bourdain was emotionally unwell. This was no secret. He became addicted to drugs early in his life, and while he was able to get treatment for his addiction, he kept his depression hidden.

In his 2000 bestseller *Kitchen Confidential*, Bourdain stated that in the various restaurants where he worked, alongside his fellow kitchen employees he used psychedelics, pharmaceuticals, amphetamines, heroin, and cocaine. During this time, he shared that he would suffer deep depression fueled by his substance abuse. "I couldn't even bear to pick up the phone. Instead, I'd just listen to the answering machine, afraid and unwilling to pick up. I was hiding, in a deep, dark hole, and it was dawning on me that it was time, really time, to try to climb out."

As his celebrity status grew, so did his influence, both as a representative of food culture and of mental health. Dr. Stephannee Standefer, who directs a master's degree program in counseling at Northwestern University, said she often used Bourdain as an example to students. She told BuzzFeed News, "We take a look at folks who are very aware of their mental health issues and concerns and who are just a couple of life events away from suicide. He's someone I used as an example of how well he articulated his awareness of his mental health."[21]

And yet Bourdain lost the battle. No one knows what goes through the mind of a person who successfully commits suicide. They aren't around to provide insight. Depression and emotional health are exceeding complex phenomena, and doctors can only do so much to diagnose and treat their patients.

---

21 BuzzFeed News. https://www.buzzfeednews.com/article/krystieyandoli/anthony-bourdain-depression-addiction-mental-illness-chef

In the past few decades, the issue of mental health in the workplace has come to the forefront. According to the CDC, poor mental health and stress can erode employee job performance and productivity, engagement, personal communications, and even physical capability and daily functioning. Mental illnesses including depression are associated with higher rates of disability and unemployment. For example, depression, which affects as many as ten percent of all Americans, can interfere with a person's ability to complete physical job tasks and reduces cognitive performance. Sadly, only fifty-seven percent of employees who report moderate depression and forty percent of those who report severe depression receive treatment to control depression symptoms.[22]

In February 2023, a sitting U.S. senator, John Fetterman of Pennsylvania, voluntarily checked himself into Walter Reed National Military Medical Center to receive treatment for clinical depression. This was a bold decision, as politicians are intensely scrutinized by the press and their political opponents for any signs of physical, mental, or emotional weakness. Senator Fetterman's wife, Gisele, said that she was "so proud of him for asking for help.... After what he's been through in the past year, there's probably no one who wanted to talk about his own health less than John. I'm so proud of him for asking for help and getting the care he needs."[23]

The response from the political and news communities was uniformly positive, with colleagues on both sides of the aisle expressing sincere hopes for his recovery and return to the Senate.

---

22 CDC. https://www.cdc.gov/workplacehealthpromotion/tools-resources/workplace-health/mental-health/index.html
23 CNN. https://www.cnn.com/2023/02/16/politics/john-fetterman-depression-treatment/index.html

As we move into the 21st century, we're becoming more open to the realities of emotional health, and we recognize that there's no stigma that should be attached to emotional health challenges. In order to become truly invaluable to your family, workplace, and community, and to *stay* invaluable for the long term, seeking professional help for emotional difficulties should be no different than getting help for a broken leg or a case of the flu.

Spiritual Health

There are many aspects to our overall well-being and ability to be invaluable, including physical, mental, and emotional health. In addition, one crucial aspect to our health that cannot be overlooked is spiritual.

The general definition of spiritual health is the embrace of your life's meaning and purpose, as well as consistency in your values and your actions, directed toward a positive, altruistic goal. A spiritually healthy person has a clear purpose in life and is able to reflect on the meaning of events in the context of striving for the betterment of others.

The qualification that spiritual health must, by definition, be *selfless* is non-negotiable. This is because a person can know their life's meaning and purpose, be consistent in their values and actions, and nonetheless be thoroughly evil and self-centered. History is full of such people—dictators and tyrants and fraudsters who gleefully leave a path of destruction and misery in their wake. They may possess the requisite knowledge, skills, attitude, physical health, and stamina to be invaluable, and yet they become the opposite: infamous for their wrongdoing.

Without spiritual health, a person could use all of his or her talents and abilities for unhealthy outcomes.

For the purposes of this book, aside from the occasional human weaknesses to which we are all subject, we're going to assume that when given the choice, you, as a good person, will always seek to be invaluable for altruistic purposes, even when those actions result in your personal financial success. We believe that good people deserve to enjoy a good life and that material rewards will flow to the person who is invaluable to others.

5. Strength

Because it's something we all struggle with, human weakness is the subject of great books, legendary movies, and even the daily gossip around the water cooler. Weakness often explains why someone's life has taken a wrong turn or why we make poor decisions that we later regret. Why do we talk about the mistakes and weaknesses of others? Because our own weaknesses are often what we fear or struggle with the most in our lives. Think about how many times you hear the expression, "I did it in a moment of weakness," to explain away an impulse reaction, extravagant purchase, eating binge, or some other sort of temptation gone wrong.

The issue with weakness is that most people interpret it as something inferior, when in reality weakness is a gift when we allow it to teach us about ourselves. Weakness, more than anything, can deliver us to strength, but only if we submit to it.

Many of the greatest things on earth have been humbled to become what they are. Steel is heated and additives introduced to become more refined and stronger. Gold is restructured to become a piece of jewelry. These metals are literally refined to make them into the building and ornamental materials we value so much. When in their apparent moment of weakness, most frequently a state of being heated, steel and gold become stronger rather than weaker. Rather than dissolve never to return to what it once was, they remain intact by flowing through the experience. Likewise, as human beings, we are called to react to what life throws our way in the heat of the moment without breaking down. We won't stop experiencing stress, which is often generated from our weaknesses; it is all about how we learn how to flow or bend and continue growing, becoming something better and stronger as a result.

Ultimately, weakness is a transitional state between a state of imperfection and toward a more valuable and beautiful state. This relationship of weakness and strength are the two sides of a coin. It is up to each of us to flip the weaknesses we encounter, and through our own mindset, flip them into strength. This is true regarding every aspect we encounter in life from our self, our body, others' words, or situations we encounter that may be out of our control.

Is weakness going to drag you down or are you going to learn from your weakness and use it to achieve something greater? We can grow from a state of failure or struggle and turn that weakness into something great. Elite athletes and performers learn how to take the challenge that weakness presents and use it correctly rather than as a threat. Supporting the alchemy of weakness into greatness doesn't mean you'll never experience weakness again or even that you'll get rid of the situation in which you feel weak. Rather, you change your mindset.

Weakness, more than anything, is an *opportunity*. The strength it takes to convert any weakness into a strength or positive outcome is based in our purpose, values, vision, mission, and goals we are striving to achieve. It is based in our ongoing growth of knowledge, skills, and developing attitude alongside our mental and physical health. Strength emanates from our mental, physical, and emotional support we provide to ourselves through all the elements we have covered in the development of our health, strength, and worth. We enable ourselves to optimize outcomes through our willitude and navigotiational capabilities.

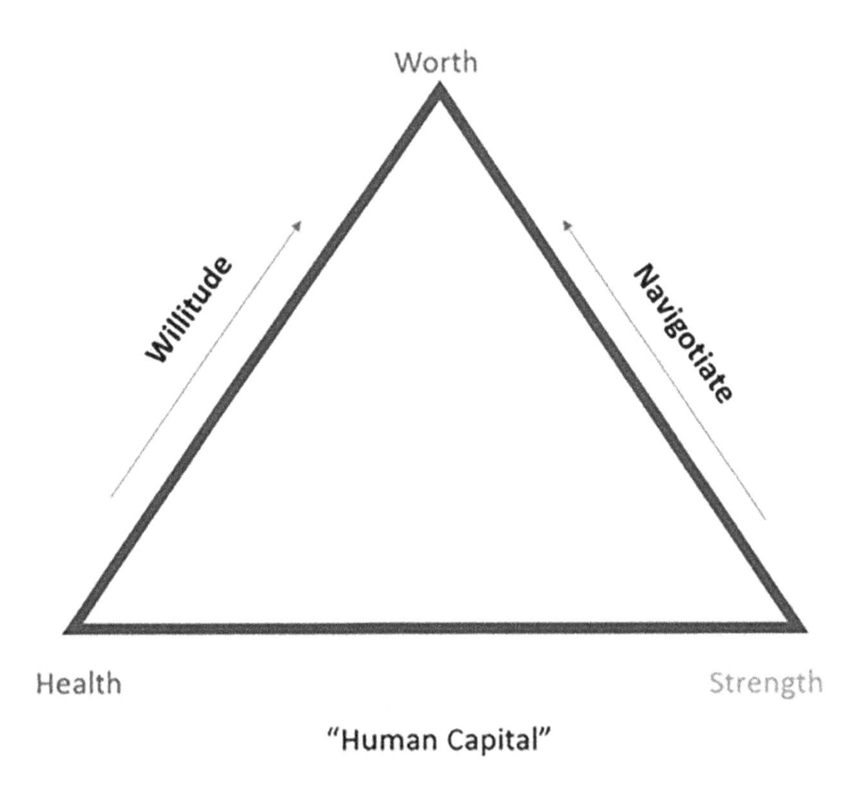

The Anatomy of Strength and Weakness

Weakness and its nominal opposite, strength, appear in many different guises, varying from one person to the next and even from one moment in our lives to another.

If each of us is made up of four elements—the mental, emotional, spiritual, and physical—then weakness can occur in any of these capacities.

A mental weakness might be the inability to stay focused or avoid distractions. Most people who struggle with distraction often carry a more creative aspect to their personality; they look at things in ways other people don't. Terry thinks of his son, Brayden, this way. Brayden is constantly looking around and finding and researching things that stimulate him. For someone who struggles with too much distraction, or lack of ability to stay focused, we would advise them to embrace this energy but go from one thing to another in a more planned and consistent manner. Think of it this way. We all need time to get things completed, and multitasking is a fallacy. If you do anything for more than ninety minutes, you may begin to flatline, because we're designed to rest and recover our energy levels throughout our daily activities. Those who struggle with distractions simply need more frequent pit stops to keep running well and focused.

For children, it's important to find the learning model that works for them. Our society trains children to learn the same way, but not everybody learns by sitting in a classroom, looking at the chalkboard and listening to the teacher. Some kids need to touch and experience objects and end up getting distracted because of this difference in learning aptitude. Good teachers use different teaching modalities for different children, subtly, so they absorb the information as equals.

An example of an emotional weakness is someone who cares so much about people that they're constantly enabling them to stay in unhealthy or unproductive situations. These are the people who clean up other people's messes, whether for their children, spouse, friends, or other family members. They put up with irresponsible behavior or hurtful words and actions and tend to make excuses for the other person. The problem is when you enable people, you are actually hurting them, not to mention hurting yourself and diverting focus from what you want and need. People who help too much usually lack boundaries—they don't know what's too much. But if this tendency is converted into a strength, for instance, if you become a psychologist, you can help people in a healthy way. As long as you do it with the proper boundaries and self-awareness, it can be a great catalyst to becoming invaluable.

A spiritual weakness plays on what we believe and how we believe it. An example would be an individual who only sees the best or worst in everyone. Believing in people's goodness is a wonderful trait, and we may have too little of it in general. However, the reality is that not everybody intends to do their best, so the weakness becomes, "I'm always getting burned." The strength could come from a different state of awareness. "I'm not always going to get burned, because I've balanced my belief with an acceptance that not everyone is always going to act out of goodness. There are some people who are going to respond to me badly no matter what I do."

The most tangible example of weakness is a physical weakness. My son, Brandon, was physically weak his entire life because he was confined to a wheelchair and could do very little on his own. Most people would interpret that as total weakness, but he was one of the strongest people I knew. His weakness taught him to be tough. Even though he couldn't physically do anything, he learned to use his charisma to get what he wanted. He did it all the time, and people didn't even know it.

We were once in a mall walking around and came across three teenage girls. Brandon was looking at them and, before you know it, they walked up to him and said, "Look how cute he is! Brandon looked small for his age, at that time maybe the size of a seven or eight-year-old, even though he was twenty-two. Before long, these girls were kneeling down and touching his hand. And all the while, Brandon's looking at them smiling and thinking, *You girls are beautiful, and I still got your attention in a wheelchair!* How many guys would love to have a group of three girls walk up and ask, "Hi, how are you?" Other people may have seen Brandon's handicap as total weakness, but the way he responded to it changed that assumption.

Whatever kind of weakness and whatever the specifics to your individual life, a single truth remains. If you take those things that you cannot change and convert them into inspiration, it will help you move through them quicker. You initiate the conversion process by deciding you will be challenged by weakness versus threatened by it. This helps you to transform bad stress into good stress and your weaknesses into strengths.

Think of the caterpillar. It's a small and rather strange insect that, when it's time to transform itself, spins itself into a chrysalis and, little does it know, comes forth later as a beautiful butterfly. The metamorphosis of caterpillar into a butterfly could not have taken place if the caterpillar wasn't up for the transformation. Through an instinctual genetic awareness of this transformation and without knowing what is to come, after the caterpillar begins its transformation through the chrysalis, it emerges as the creature it's meant to be—more beautiful and more adapted to survive and thrive. So, is a butterfly an improved caterpillar? Or is it its own thing? It's a butterfly that came from the transformation of the caterpillar self!

Like the caterpillar changing into the butterfly, you can transform yourself into a person of high self-worth.

Every religion believes there has to be a death to atone for life. Let your old self go, let the past flow under the bridge of life and move forward, (learning from the past), and stepping into a new version of yourself with greater capabilities. Weakness is the human classroom for our potential transformation into greatness.

A Lazy Mind Is the Devil's Workshop

When I was growing up, my mom would say to me, "A lazy mind is the devil's workshop!" And while she may have been referring to my laziness about chores, it can be broadened to include a mental laziness about helping ourselves throughout our lives. If we sit idle and wait for things to change, chances are they're only going to get worse.

The paradox of the weakness-to-strength process is that we all feel weakness at times. The goal isn't to eliminate weakness but rather to not get stuck in it. The real question is how long you'll stay there. Weakness is always there to teach us a lesson, but there is a critical period for action. If we don't act, we might miss our opportunity and drift into apathy, anger, regret, or self-pity. We might get stuck if we don't *discover* what weakness is meant to teach us. Linearity is the problem, not the emotion itself. Weakness asks us to understand what it is, to allow it to educate us as much as possible, then to ask a better question. Instead of, "Why me?" we should ask, "How can I convert this to help me? How can I use this to get what I really want out of life?" Otherwise, we flatline—mentally, emotionally, spiritually, and physically—and fail to learn the lessons of weakness.

The need for action can be met, paradoxically, by surrendering ourselves to something or someone else. We must yield and lean into weakness by becoming servants in order for that to happen. The Bible states: "He that is great among you shall be your servant." Dr. Martin Luther King, Jr., echoed a similar sentiment in his "I Have A Dream" speech. He said the fight for equality wasn't about violence and aggression but attitude. He knew the equal rights movement needed to be done in the right way, with passion. That's what made his speech so resounding at that point in history—he knew they were standing at a moment of potential greatness but had to respond correctly.

Terry, in serving his son, Brandon, learned how to become strong. He learned that it's not just about brute strength but also about finesse. It's how to speak, using body language, tone of voice, and other skills born out of his experiences with Brandon.

Many people might interpret being subservient to a person or a thing as weakness, but in reality the greatest way to help someone is to serve them. It's also the greatest way to help yourself.

Servitude Is Fortitude

A good example of the power of servitude is in our intimate relationships. Women or men who exhibit power under control, keeping power in check, rather than overpowering the other to get what they want are much more successful in the long run. It's all about serving another, in this example a man serving a woman, until she comes to you; eventually she'll tell you what she wants and needs, enabling you to give it to her.

What about Mother Teresa, you may ask? She was selfless, altruistic, and dedicated her life to helping others. And yet she died a pauper. What about that?

The answer is that like many selfless people, Mother Teresa *chose* to live in poverty, at least as most of us define it. As the founder of the Missionaries of Charity, she had a few choice words to say about the meaning of the word "poverty." She said, "In the developed countries there is a poverty of intimacy, a poverty of spirit, of loneliness, of lack of love. There is no greater sickness in the world today than that one." And also, "Poverty in the West is a different kind of poverty. It is not only a poverty of loneliness but also of spirituality. There's a hunger for love, as there is a hunger for God."[24]

There are many leaders of charitable organizations who choose not to live in poverty. For example, Insher Ashing is the head of Save the Children, a respected global charity with annual revenue of over $2 billion that operates across 122 countries. In 2020, her salary was $250,553. Ashing has been a member of Save the Children since 1998, first as a youth advocate and then as a member. She's earned every penny she makes, and in the scheme of things, her take-home pay is far less than many CEOs of for-profit companies of comparable revenues.[25]

So the question is moot, because with her extraordinary knowledge, skills, attitude, health, and strength, Mother Teresa could have taken the road to material comfort. She became invaluable, and yet she deliberately chose to lead a simple life.

Religion and spirituality are not synonymous. Some people find their spiritual health in practicing religion, while others do not. There is no right or wrong way to achieve spiritual health—it's whatever works for you.

Some ways that may help you elevate your spiritual health include:

Helping others. Most people derive a sense of wellbeing when they're of service to others. This can take on many forms, including being a positive influence at work, volunteering at a charity, offering a hand to a friend in need, or simply being kind to strangers.

Being in nature. Some people feel very connected and at peace when they are walking outdoors or outside of the city. Being in an environment where you, the human, are relative-

24 https://www.quotesgeeks.com/mother-teresa-quotes-on-poverty/
25 https://kiiky.com/wealth/highest-paid-nonprofit-ceos/

ly unimportant is both humbling and awe-inspiring. You can get the same feeling by gazing up at a starry sky, toward the horizon of the ocean, or at a distant mountain range; or the opposite—watching close-up the activities of a beehive or ant colony that does not depend upon human interaction.

Gratitude. There are many things in this world that help to sustain us—our food, our shelter, our friends, our good health. They all deserve our gratitude. Many people find they feel the most connected to a sense of spirituality when they feel grateful. You may even make a weekly list of all the things you're grateful for or say a "thank you" out loud for all you have.

The Intersection Between Mental and Physical Strength

To maintain or improve your physical strength requires the mental strength to endure the development of muscle and aerobic fitness. Hence, the really important form of strength is mental strength. It's the kind demonstrated by Stephen Hawking and many others who stay laser-focused on what they want to accomplish to make themselves invaluable to their community. It's shown by the kid who grows up in a crime-ridden slum or an impoverished rural town and who sets his or her sights on leading a successful life.

Mental strength is really emotional resiliency, which is the ability to cope with stress and challenges in a healthy way. It has nothing to do with mental disease or defect; many people with a diagnosed mental illness have learned to manage their condition in a healthy way and have cultivated strong emotional resilience.

Our mental strength helps us resist being thrown off course by negative thoughts and helps us stay on track to becoming invaluable, day after day. It's the cognitive and emotional skill of reframing adverse circumstances and negative thoughts. Being mentally strong helps us resist both internal and external influences that weaken our self-confidence and well-being.

As Thomas Jefferson said, "Nothing can stop the man with the right mental attitude from achieving his goal; nothing on earth can help the man with the wrong mental attitude." While having mental and emotional strength is a *prerequisite* for becoming invaluable, it can be acquired through adversity. If your goal means something to you, then you'll discover an untapped well of mental strength that you may not have realized you had. You can add to the depth of this well through physical fitness. How many stories have we heard of ordinary people, who never thought of themselves as having any special powers, being put under duress and then showing tremendous mental strength?

You can develop your mental strength by focusing on the positive and not dwelling on the negative.

- Don't waste time feeling sorry for yourself. Take responsibility for your life, even the parts where you think you got shortchanged or were victimized.

- Keep your power. You cannot control what other people do, but you can—and must—control what you do and how you behave under pressure.

- Embrace inevitable change. Nothing lasts forever. If a change is beyond your control, then roll with it.

- Don't try to please everyone. Be willing to say "no" when you need to. You cannot solve every problem in the world or make every person happy.

- Stay focused on the future. The past is gone. You cannot change it, but you can learn from it. Constantly reliving bad experiences is just as damaging as fantasizing about the old glory days. Live for the present and plan for the future.

- Make mistakes once, not twice. Accept responsibility for your decisions and learn from your past mistakes. If one solution fails, try another one. Move on and make better decisions in the future.

When you're invaluable, the people around you depend on you for your inner strength. Don't try to be Superman, but always keep your positive power charged and ready!

Invaluable Spotlight Profile: Dr. Ginger Decker

Dr. Ginger Decker is a Real Health Educator, Clean Health & Beauty Product Formulator, author, and international speaker who's been featured on the Dr. Oz Show, WebMD, and major networks.

When her father passed away from cancer, she realized that she wanted to become invaluable by teaching people about health and wellness. She learned and currently teaches that if you give your body the proper tools like nutrition and getting rid of toxins, then it knows what to do to stay healthy.

She turned all her education toward formulating clean health and beauty products. She teaches that for real health, you want to boost your immune system with clean real nutrition and lower your body's toxic load.

Her mission is to give people hope and teach real health.

In 2001, when she lived in Florida, she was asked to be a part of a charity event to climb Mount Denali in Alaska. It took thirty-one days up and down, due to having to wait out a few storms. One of the biggest challenges was going to be the high altitude, so she ordered a device from a company called Hypoxico and would sleep with the device in a tent five weeks prior to her trip to try and help with altitude sickness. Failure was not an option, and this invaluable experience taught her more about pushing herself mentally than anything else she's ever done.

THE BOTTOM LINE!

- Know and develop the five personal attributes in building your worth: knowledge, skills, attitude, health, and strength.

  1. The knowledge you have about the world or a subject or a skill set consists of the facts and information you've acquired through education, professional training, or experience.

  2. Our skills are what you do with your knowledge. It's the learned ability to produce acceptable results with good execution, often within a given amount of time, energy, or both. Skills come in two general categories—hard skills and soft skills.

  3. Attitude is what you feel about your knowledge and skills reflected in their behavior. It's all about whether you want to leverage these attributes to become invaluable or take them for granted and, for whatever reason, fail to exploit them.

  4. Good health is one key to becoming invaluable, because the healthier you are, the happier and more positive you tend to be. If nature provided you with a functioning, healthy body, then you owe it to yourself to take good care of it. Mental health, physical health, and your ability to be a fully contributing member of society are inexorably linked.

  5. Physical strength is good, essential for sustained mental performance, but the really important form of strength is mental strength. It's the kind demonstrat-

ed by people who stay laser-focused on what they want to accomplish to make themselves invaluable to their community. Your mental strength helps you resist being thrown off course by negative thoughts and helps you stay on track to becoming invaluable, day after day.

- As Thomas Jefferson said, "Nothing can stop the man with the right mental attitude from achieving his goal; nothing on earth can help the man with the wrong mental attitude."
- When you're invaluable, the people around you depend on you for your inner strength. Don't get pulled off track!

VISION, MISSION, AND SERVANT LEADERSHIP

Vision

Vision is looking ahead to see an outcome you truly envision for yourself and those around you. Some experts suggest looking out ten years while others feel it is hard to see further than three to five years ahead in today's fast-changing world. We subscribe to the ten-year view of developing your vision statement in order to reach further than you might typically imagine. When you stretch your thoughts in this fashion, you enable your brain to process both the emotional and logical aspects of achieving this vision. When you write out your vision, you should state it in present tense terms, as if it has happened. This present tense of something ten years out is how we empower ourselves to clearly see the outcome and take the necessary action steps to reach our vision every day.

Looking and seeing are very different things. Looking can be a glance or a ponder visually, but seeing is focusing on an object or direction that can determine purposeful success.

Psalm 119:105 reads, "Thy word is a lamp unto my feet, and a light unto my path."

Simply stated, vision needs to be both short term and long term to stay on the projected course without falling into a short-term ditch. The lamp was the light of that day, which would be ultimate at the walking level (short term vision and concentration), while the light when held up is to see down range (medium and long-term vision and concentration). Both short and long-range perspectives are necessary to develop the desired results that vision brings to the mission and goals success.

In our vision, we are focused on the long-term path, seeing and visualizing this outcome we believe in fully. Vision differs from purpose in that your purpose and your values remain the same and do not change. Your vision, on the other hand, evolves over time. It doesn't change every year, but your vision statement is likely to morph over several years as you move forward toward your vision. The key portion of this evolution is establishing and accomplishing your mission along the way.

Mission

In our definition of becoming invaluable, your mission is what you must accomplish in the next twelve months toward achieving your ten-year vision. Mission is the short and medium-term light. The mission statement is written once you have clearly established your measurable goals or objectives for the year ahead. Write them down, and please make all goals or objectives SMART (specific, measurable, achievable, relevant, and time-based) in order to hold yourself accountable. Once you have three to five critical goals or objectives, use these statements to craft your mission statement—again, what you must accomplish in the next twelve months.

A mission is a specific task with which a person or group is charged. As this definition states, the mission is all about the execution of a projected vision to ascertain preset goals. Since goals are measurable, mission execution is critical to determine specific achievements with accountability for overall mission success.

What is your mission to become invaluable? Do you have a purpose (why), a vision seeing yourself fulfilling that purpose, and then how do you make it your reality, through mission execution for optimal success? These are all basic but profound steps to becoming invaluable in your own life every day.

Great performers make a plan and then work the plan to completion without excuses, aiming to not become a victim but rather a champion! Champions start every day doing the same rituals to complete another day with a championship mindset.

Once you have a ten-year vision and a one-year mission with specific goals and objectives, you can carry this short-term vision, your mission, forward toward the ten-year mark by thinking about a mission two, three, even perhaps four and five years out. In other words, you are establishing potential goals and objectives for up to five years. All of these goals, objectives, and the mission get revisited each year and continuously evolve as you reach or fall short of the accomplishment of your mission in respect to your long-term vision.

As we move forward to implement all we are suggesting, let's take a moment to reflect on all we have explored. You should now have a written purpose, set of values, a ten-year vision statement, and have established the goals and objectives for the next twelve months, leading to a concise mission statement. We have explored the ongoing development of knowledge, applying that knowledge through our developing skills with a positive, can-do attitude. We have discussed the aspects of mental and physical health, and the development of strength, the resilient flexibility one develops when of sound mind and body. All of these attributes enable you to have incredible willitude to navigotiate your way through all challenges or obstacles to achieve your vision in a purposeful and principled fashion. All of our discussion is about leadership of yourself, which enables you to lead others in an even more successful fashion.

Servant Leadership

Before we move ahead to the practicalities of achieving your vision in a purposeful and principled fashion, we need to discuss how you're going to do that in regard to your relationship with the people to whom you hope to become invaluable.

By this we mean, what will be your approach? How can you get people to recognize your value and the influence you may develop with them?

You cannot go in like a military general and announce, "I'm here to help you! You're going to love what I do for you!" Unless you're a teacher talking to your class of third-graders, that's not going to work.

The approach that works best—in nearly any situation—is *servant leadership*.

The goal of servant leadership is to help another person or a group to attain a common goal by *serving* them. By this we mean you help them set a goal and then you provide the direction and assistance necessary so they can reach that goal through their own effort. Your helping hand is not exactly invisible, but it's unobtrusive. In fact, it is exactly what we are trying to do through *Becoming Invaluable*—to serve you in your life's journey and greatly enhance your cnjoyment and outcomes.

It's an ancient concept, first articulated by the Chinese philosopher Lao-tsu in the 6th century BCE. Chapter 17 of his *Tao-te Ching* is frequently cited by Western scholars as the earliest concept of servant leadership expressing the ideals of listening to others, putting their concerns first, and thereby becoming almost invisible to them:

"A leader is best when people barely know that he exists. Not so good when people obey and acclaim him. Worst when they despise him. But of a good leader, who talks little, when his work is done, his aim fulfilled, they will all say, 'We did this ourselves.'"

Another quote expressing the same concept comes from Nelson Mandela in his autobiography, *Long Walk to Freedom*: "He stays behind the flock, letting the most nimble go out ahead, whereupon the others follow, not realizing that all along they are being directed from behind."

In the business world, the concept of servant leadership was most widely popularized by Robert K. Greenleaf. While working for AT&T (then the American Telephone and Telegraph Company) during the 1950s, he felt a growing suspicion that the top-down authoritarian leadership style prominent in American companies was not working, and in 1964 he took an early retirement to found the Greenleaf Center for Servant Leadership. He used the term "servant leadership" in "The Servant as Leader," an essay he first published in 1970. He wrote:

"The servant-leader is servant first... It begins with the natural feeling that one wants to serve, to serve first. Then conscious choice brings one to aspire to lead. That person is sharply different from one who is leader first, perhaps because of the need to assuage an unusual power drive or to acquire material possessions...The leader-first and the servant-first are two extreme types. Between them there are shadings and blends that are part of the infinite variety of human nature."[26]

Servant leadership can be used in any situation—even in the military. It may surprise you to know that in the US Marine

26 Greenleaf. https://www.greenleaf.org/what-is-servant-leadership/

Corps, servant leadership is a core concept. It's called "service-based leadership," and the goal is to prioritize your team's physical and emotional needs before your own. This is where the dictum "officers eat last" comes from, and it's literally true. Officers in the chow line wait to be served until all Marines beneath them in rank have gotten their food. Much like parents with their children, they feed the young first to ensure the next wave of leadership development. The rule creates a sense of unity and instills loyalty, and it's an attitude that more business leaders should adopt.

It's also very useful as a management tool. In many units, the most senior Marines present actually serve their subordinates. This selfless act shows the Marines that their leadership cares about them. And if the food runs out, the officers would be the ones to go without eating. But it also gives the leaders the opportunity to see and talk to all of the Marines as they file through the chow line. With this up-close contact, officers can assess their troops' physical and mental wellbeing and if necessary take steps to improve it.

Servant leadership is the best and most powerful way to become invaluable to another person or a group. Let's say you're a manager at work. Sitting in your office and issuing memos and orders is the *worst* way to be a leader and the *quickest* way to make yourself irrelevant in the eyes of your subordinates.

What should you do? Get out and walk around the shop or office. Show that you're ready, available, and engaged. Do this at random times during the day. When you walk through the workplace, smile. Greet your employees and ask about their families—the kids, weekend plans, an upcoming vacation. Above all, ask if they need any help completing a task or reaching a goal. Compliment them in public for a job well done. Offer feedback in private.

Another important aspect to leadership is those being led always watch the leader for cues and information. The leader's character is tested in this manner. Does he or she sacrifice their own comfort to accomplish the mission? Do they forgo comforts the workers do not have? And, perhaps most importantly, do they keep their word? This might be the most important thing they watch for and is demonstrated by their behavior in front of the workers.

Of course there are privileges to rank; everyone recognizes this, and employees don't begrudge their leadership these traditions. But when the going gets tough, the privileges need to disappear. This thinking applies to the successful artist or parent just the same as the military or business leader. Those around you need to see the willitude in sacrifices made and through overcoming obstacles while having the ability to navigotiate through the many different types of people and situations one might encounter.

As I am sure you can imagine, it requires a great deal of discipline and effort to consistently develop the knowledge, skills, and experience while building your health and strength foundation to possess such willitude and navigotiation abilities. We will take a look at the methodology we have found successful in the next chapters.

Invaluable Spotlight Profile: Jennifer Potter-Brotman

Jennifer Potter-Brotman has over thirty years of experience in senior operating roles in professional services companies. Most recently, she ran the Boston office of Russell Reynolds, a global leader in assessment, recruitment, and succession planning. Her former roles include working in private equity and serving as president and CEO of the Forum Corporation, a leader in corporate training and education.

From an early age, being the oldest child in her family put her in a position of heightened responsibility. This had a huge impact on her; her grandmother and her mother were both very strong women.

She's always worked in the field of human capital and spent over twenty years in a leadership development firm, beginning as an editor and ultimately following the founder as CEO. When the leadership development firm was sold to a large publishing firm just before 9/11, she became CEO, following the founder. Her manager at the parent company had a different view of how to run the business, and eventually Jennifer went to the founder and said she could not be in that environment anymore and needed to get out.

Her choices have paid off. The last six years have been amazing because everything she's doing now is what she wants to do. She's someone who strives to be invaluable, wants to keep learning, and prioritizes having an impact while doing her best work.

THE BOTTOM LINE!

- Vision is looking ahead to see an outcome you truly envision for yourself and those around you.
- We subscribe to the ten-year view of developing your vision statement. Write out your vision and state it in present tense terms, as if it has happened.
- Your vision can evolve over time.
- Your mission is what you must accomplish in the next twelve months toward achieving your ten-year vision.
- Write your mission statement once you have clearly established your measurable goals or objectives for the year ahead. Make all goals or objectives SMART (specific, measurable, achievable, relevant, and time-based) in order to hold yourself accountable.
- At this point in your journey to becoming invaluable, you should have a written purpose, set of values, and a ten-year vision statement, and have established the goals and objectives for the next twelve months leading you to a concise mission statement.
- To achieve your vision in a purposeful and principled fashion, use the principle of servant leadership. It's the best and most powerful way to become invaluable to another person or a group.

6 YOUR DAILY HEALTH AND STRENGTH BUILDER

On rising in the morning, you need to begin your day with mental, emotional, spiritual, and physical strength. If you can start on this footing every day and maintain it day after day, you'll eventually find yourself being invaluable to others, even without consciously being aware of your progress. Because you can deliver results, other people will increasingly depend on you for solutions, support, and answers, and you'll find that you can provide these things. You'll feel as though *you* haven't changed, but the world and its people have gotten increasingly simpler and in need of guidance that you can provide.

Creating sustained progress with your Daily Strength Builder will take work. Happy work, we hope, but work nonetheless. It will be happy work because you'll know it's for a good cause and that you'll reap the benefits, just as you're helping others benefit too. It's work that needs to be done according to a steady, disciplined schedule.

For Steve, perhaps the most influential book of the many he has read is a very short volume called *In the Sphere of Silence,* by Vijay Eswaran. The goal of the book is to show you how to slow down and take stock of where you are and where you are headed. The book's central message can be summed up as: listen a lot, think before you speak, and make to-do lists daily. The practice includes a one-hour period of reflection that teaches you how to be still and examine what is within yourself. It's divided into three paths: Duty, Knowledge, and Reflection. Duty looks at the goals and tasks you must work to achieve. Knowledge focuses on self-improvement and learning. Reflection ensures the practitioner spends time on mindfulness.[27]

The mental side of your Daily Strength Builder in the pages ahead is developed from this book and others. It's an example of continuous learning in developing your capacity to be invaluable.

Yes, it requires a high degree of discipline to use the first two hours of your day to set yourself up for success. We recommend practicing your Daily Strength Builder from four to six days per week. Each day of practice, you can do either the mental or the physical first. What's important are routine and consistency.

People often will say to you throughout the day, "How are you today?" Our preferred way to answer is to say, "I don't know, but I have the next seventeen (or whatever the number) hours to figure out how to make it the greatest day of my life!"

27 https://www.inthesphereofsilence.com/

Your first two hours set the stage to help make it a great day—and then a great week, month, and year. You use those two hours for mental and physical fitness, planning, and daily action.

Here's our Daily Strength Builder plan. Adapt it to make it your own, and then stick to it as a personal commitment.

Hour One: Prepare Your Mind and Spirit

Here's our suggested schedule for the first hour of your day.

10 minutes: Meditate.

10 minutes: Review goals and visualizing achieving them.

10 minutes: Write and review your weekly to-do list.

15 minutes: Read for knowledge development.(Reading is preferred and reiterated in the following pages. Some people prefer listening to an Audio Book versus reading, if while maintaining full focus on the learning this can work.)

5 minutes: Take notes from your reading or listening.

10 minutes: Engage in prayer or spiritual contemplation.

Meditate

Start your day with a clear mind and heart. Research has shown that morning meditation can improve mindfulness and reduce negative feelings of anxiety and depression. Everyone knows how to worry, and worry is negative meditation! Simply change the object of focus to a positive image for it to become a healthy meditation. It allows you to detach and sit peacefully above your thoughts while you get acquainted with your higher self. You give yourself the best opportunity to be fully awake, fully aware, and fully alive before "doing" anything. You can use positive mental imagery for visualization, and as you develop your ability to visualize and feel positive emotions in the process, this will influence and attract more positive circumstances in your future.

You can meditate while sitting in one position, while doing yoga, or while walking. It can be done sitting on a pillow on the floor, riding in a taxi, sitting in the airport, or while waiting for your breakfast smoothie to blend. Everyone has their own preferred environment that best facilitates meditation, but it should be very simple and comfortable. It's not about trying to build a complicated morning routine—it's about quality, ritual, and the motivation to get started.

You can use guided or unguided meditation. Guided meditation is led by an instructor who directs you step-by-step through your meditation experience. If you're meditating at home, this would be either pre-recorded or accessed online. Unguided meditation is practiced without external instructions, and you lead yourself through your own meditations.

Steve once had a friend who lived at the end of a long driveway. Every morning, rain or shine, he would walk from his house to the mailbox at the end of the driveway. He'd take the newspaper from the mailbox and then walk back to the house. The round trip took him about ten minutes, but walking through the morning air gave him a chance to connect with nature, clear his mind, and just enjoy being alive. He also got a nice bit of aerobic exercise!

You can meditate in the shower in the morning, as long as you have no distractions. Focus on the sensation of the water streaming over the top of your head and down to your feet. Imagine the water washing away any stress, tension, and worry from the body and mind. Enjoy the sound of the rushing water and the trickling of the drain. Indulge in the moment by closing your eyes as you stand under the water. The shower meditation is ideal if you're short on time, as it does not take any extra minutes from your day; it's a good way to incorporate present-moment awareness into your routine.

However you choose to do it, pick a room or outdoor area free from excessive noise or distractions. If you're inside or have earbuds, you can play your favorite relaxing background music.

Daily meditation is a key part of your Daily Strength Builder. Set an appointment with yourself and use a timer or the alarm on your phone. This will help you from feeling anxious about the time.

To release tension, start your daily meditation practice with some long and slow deep breaths. If you're walking, just keep a steady pace and breathe from your diaphragm. Either focus your mind on a mantra or just let the thoughts pass in and out without attaching any feelings to them.

Review Your Goals and Visualize Achieving Them

The three primary reasons why people fail to achieve their goals are because they forget about a goal a few weeks after setting it, they get distracted by other opportunities and ideas, and they don't take consistent action toward their goal. Fortunately, there's a simple way to overcome these reasons for failure.

Review your goals every morning. A daily checkup on your goals reveals incremental progress, but it also keeps you going forward rather than just showing how far you've come. It acts as a daily motivation to remind you why you selected this goal and the great satisfaction derived from achieving it in the end. Assessing your goals every day reminds you that the only way to get to your goals is to keep going. You cannot get that promotion by only dreaming of getting it!

Even better, write down your goals. A study from Dominican University revealed that people who did that accomplished more than those who did not. The study also showed that people who kept track of their progress at least once per week accomplished significantly more than those who didn't.[28]

Be sure to visualize your goals in clear terms. This is a simple technique that helps you create a vivid mental image of a positive future event. By using visualization, you can practice in advance of the event so that you can prepare for it and build the self-confidence you need to perform well. You're literally training your mind for a successful outcome.

We'll talk much more about visualization in chapter 8, but here's the quick introduction to this very important topic. Begin by knowing what you want to focus on. Pick one goal to start visualizing. For example, visualize a successful outcome to the product launch next week. Start imagining the exact scene. Be as clear as possible—the more specific you are and the more details you imagine, the better the visualization will work for you. Imagine the product flying off the store shelves or your delivery team rushing to fulfill more orders. You can even write down in one or two sentences the goal you have achieved in your visualization, and post it where you can see it. The more you make success part of the everyday fabric of your life, the more invaluable you'll become.

Write and Review Your Weekly To-Do List

In order to reach any goal, after visualizing that goal you need to take a series of specific steps to make it a reality. These steps need to be recorded in a to-do list. A daily review of that list is an opportunity to direct your life with intention, think

28 https://sidsavara.com/wp-content/uploads/2008/09/researchsummary2.pdf

about the past few days, reflect on what went well and what didn't, and plan for the day or week ahead.

For example, let's say that in your quest to become invaluable, you've offered to give a presentation at your local business roundtable meeting. Let's say that your area of expertise is recycling, and you intend to tell the assembled group how their businesses can get involved. Today is Monday, and the meeting is Thursday morning. That gives you three days to prepare. On Monday, your to-do list might include a review of presentations you've given in the past, and how well they went (or didn't go!). Tuesday's task might be to research new developments in the field of recycling. On Wednesday, you'll write or revise your speech and rehearse it. On Thursday, you'll deliver it. On Friday, you'll see what kind of feedback you've gotten.

Each daily task must be substantive enough to be meaningful while small enough so that you can actually get it done. You never want to set a goal and try to cram all the necessary steps into a short amount of time! And some goals include steps that must be spaced apart because of circumstances that are out of your control. For example, let's say your project is enrolling in a master's degree program. To do this, you'll need to adhere to the calendar set by the college or university.

Speaking of calendars, be sure to use your digital calendar to help you organize the tasks on your to-do list. For every task you have to get done, estimate how long it will take and block that time period off in advance. This method will help you better prioritize your work, give you built-in deadlines, and remind you when it's time to get it done.

When you complete a task, check it off your list. This simple act will make you feel good. We mean that literally! When you give that task a big checkmark, your brain releases a bit of dopamine, a neurotransmitter responsible for generating feelings of satisfaction, accomplishment, and happiness. This release of dopamine also motivates you to continue completing tasks and extending that good feeling.

Read for Knowledge Development

In our hectic workaday world, and especially with digital devices that deliver tiny nuggets of dubious "news" to our brains 'round the clock, it's very important to take fifteen minutes—or more—every day to read quality newspapers and books that convey substantive, useful information.

We hate to sound like aging boomers, but in the old days everyone in business started their day by reading one or more daily newspapers, delivered to their home at dawn by the local paperboy. Every city and town had its own newspaper, and in fifteen minutes at the breakfast table you could get a good overview of the important events of the day.

Sadly, most local papers have disappeared, but you can still find the big national papers. And luckily, most of them are now online. You can open your laptop and scroll through *The New York Times, The Wall Street Journal, USA Today*, and even foreign papers like *The Times of India,* which happens to be the largest circulated English-language daily newspaper in the world.

Perhaps the most famous newspaper reader in America is Warren Buffett, who has described his job as mainly reading with an occasional investment decision. He told an interviewer, "I read and read and read. I probably read five to six hours a day. I don't read as fast now as when I was younger. But I read five daily newspapers. I read a fair number of magazines. I read 10-Ks. I read annual reports. I read a lot of other things, too. I've always enjoyed reading."[29]

---

29 https://fs.blog/warren-buffett-information/

In addition to reading news publications, you can start your day by reading a book that will enrich you and help you lead a happier life. The book you're reading now is a good one to choose! If you're new to the world of self-help books, you might start with the classics—the ones that have been read by millions of people. The list includes *Think and Grow Rich* by Napoleon Hill, *The Alchemist* by Paul Coelho, *You Can Heal Your Life* by Louise Hay, and *Rich Dad, Poor Dad* by Robert T. Kiyosaki. And let's not forget the greatest (and best-selling) self-help book of all time, the Bible.

Fiction is good too! Reading a great novel, short stories, or even poetry is a powerful way to understand others, enhance your emotional and practical intelligence, and deepen your understanding of the world. Quality works of fiction often tackle difficult subjects in ways that simple reporting on them cannot. Stories can broaden your imagination and thinking process, take you into another world, open your mind to new ideas and possibilities, and give you the opportunity to see the world through the eyes of others.

No matter what you read in the morning—news, self-help, spirituality, fiction—make sure it's of the highest quality. When you elevate your preferences, you make yourself increasingly invaluable. And remember, every time you read, you are potentially enhancing your vocabulary and command of written language.

Take Notes From Your Reading

While you're reading (thereby making a total of twenty minutes for both) or for five minutes after you read, jot down the main points of what you've read. You do this because the act of writing helps you remember what you just read, in addition to giving you notes that you can refer to later.

There is no one right way to take notes while reading. Experiment with different strategies, find some that work for you, and use them. Be sure to know *why* you are taking notes. If you're studying for an exam, your notes are going to look different than if you're reading for general knowledge. How you take notes will depend on the reason you're taking notes. Try to write by hand; research shows that students who take notes by hand, using pen and paper, tend to retain significantly more information than those who use computers.[30] It's the combination of the use of your senses and muscles that enhance your memory.

To help you focus on the main points instead of getting caught up in details, try reading short sections of your reading (a paragraph or two, up to a page) and then pausing to think about what you just read. Then make notes from your memory. This will ensure that the words you write are your own, and you're not just copying verbatim what you read. You don't need to write pages of notes—keep them brief and focused.

Your notes should include both the content of your reading, with brief summaries or paraphrasing, as well as your reaction to the content, which may include your reaction and questions you feel it raises.

Engage in Prayer or Spiritual Contemplation

Since these terms can have various meanings to different people, let's begin with some definitions.

For most people, the word "prayer" means "an act of communication by humans with the sacred or holy—God, the gods, the transcendent realm, or supernatural powers."[31] That is to say, it's the deliberate direction of speech or thought to a higher power who could presumably convey some benefit to you.

30 https://www.skillsyouneed.com/write/notes-reading.html
31 https://www.britannica.com/topic/prayer

The Oxford English Dictionary defines "contemplation" as "the action of beholding, or looking at with attention and thought... The action of contemplating or mentally viewing; the action of thinking about a thing continuously; attentive consideration, study... Without reference to a particular object: Continued thinking, meditation, musing... Sometimes, a meditation expressed in writing... Religious musing, devout meditation. (The earliest sense; very common down to 17th c.)[32]

The Center for Action and Contemplation (CAC) says it's "the practice of being fully present—in heart, mind, and body—to what is in a way that allows you to creatively respond and work toward what could be. For many, contemplation is prayer or meditation, a daily practice of deep listening to better connect with ourselves and divine love."[33]

In all cultures and religions, you find contemplation practices. Christianity defines contemplation as a state of awareness of the vision and union with God.

No matter what you call it or the form you give it, when you engage in contemplation (the term we'll use for convenience), you're doing something uniquely human. You're using your consciousness of self and your ability to reflect upon the past and imagine the future to make sense of the world around you and your place in it. Unlike meditation, which is generally thought of as *not* focusing on some aspect of life but instead observing, as if from a distance, the thoughts that enter and then exit your mind, contemplation is the active but non-judgmental exploration of some aspect of the world. In your morning contemplation, you might reflect upon the state of your career, your family, or some goal you've set for yourself. While contemplation is not an exercise in deliberate problem-solving,

32 OED. https://www.oed.com/
33 CAC. https://cac.org/about/what-is-contemplation/

through the process of contemplation, solutions and ideas may emerge. According to the Contemplative Mind in Society, contemplative practices have their roots in two intentions, "cultivating awareness and developing a stronger connection to the divine or inner wisdom."[34]

Demonstrated benefits of contemplative practices include stress reduction, improved self-regulation, enhanced attention and awareness abilities, and enhanced empathy awareness. It's related to *mindfulness*, an ancient Buddhist meditation technique used to train the mind. It's a form of mental training to improve one's ability to raise the level of awareness and intentionally direct attention. For example, if you're with your partner in the morning and you sense that he or she is irritable or depressed, and you realize that you should respond to these unspoken emotional messages, that's a form of mindfulness.

In mindfulness meditation, breathing plays an important role, as you strive to pay full attention to the present moment in order to become more aware.

In contrast, *mindlessness* is a state of reduced awareness caused by distraction, focusing only on yourself, ruminating about things that displease you, or being involved in multiple tasks so that you're not fully engaged in any of them.

As you can see, the practice of prayer and spiritual contemplation is what you make it. People have been doing it for thousands of years, and there are endless interpretations and approaches you can take. The important thing is that every morning you take ten minutes to slow down, quiet your mind, and become aware not only of your immediate surroundings but of the big picture of your life and your journey to becoming invaluable.

---

34 Johannes, Judith, "Contemplative Education: How Contemplative Practices Can Support and Improve Education" (2012). Master's Capstone Projects. 17. Retrieved from https://scholarworks.umass.edu/cie_capstones/17

Hour Two: Prepare Your Body

Having cleared your mind and created focus for the day ahead, it's now time to invigorate your body and get your heart, lungs, and muscles ready for the day. While science hasn't provided an answer as to which time of day, if any, is best for exercise, the advantage to exercising in the morning before you go to work is that you have more control over your time before the commitments of the day kick in. You're usually not asked to write a report or do errands at the crack of dawn. Friends don't invite you to a party at six o'clock in the morning!

If you don't exercise in the morning, you may not have the opportunity again during the day. Then you'll have to wait until after work, if you can fit it in.

Like meditation, exercise requires time. At this point, a certain realization may be entering your mind. "I'm going to have to get up earlier in the morning!" Yes, you may have to do that, and that means you should go to bed a little earlier too. You can look at it this way. Your Monday morning really begins on Sunday night at bedtime. If you stay up late on Sunday, you're going to impact how you feel on Monday.

To determine the time you need to get up—and therefore the time you need to go to sleep the night before—think about your morning deadline, or the time of your earliest ironclad obligation, such as arriving at the office or driving your kids to school. Then work backward. Allow time for the usual routine (getting dressed, shower, breakfast, commute) and then add the two hours you'll need to perform your Daily Strength Builder.

For those who are natural early birds, waking up a little earlier can be easy, but if you're a night owl it can be more challenging. To wake up and start a morning exercise routine, you may need to shift your entire circadian clock to be earlier. That can take time—be patient and don't force it.

Bright light helps, because it tells your body to stop making melatonin, a hormone that makes you sleepy. Being exposed to bright light in the morning is the best way to help train your circadian cycle. In the summer, a good way to feel energized is to step into the bright morning sunshine right away. In the winter, you'll probably be rising before the sun. In that case, you'll need some bright artificial light to wake up your body. And we mean *really bright*—your normal bedroom lighting delivers a small fraction of the lux that the sun does. (A lux is the measurement of light that equals one lumen falling upon one square meter.) Typical family living room lighting is one hundred lux. In contrast, direct sunlight is an average of fifty thousand lux! That amount will wake you up!

The first hour of your Daily Strength Builder is devoted to preparing your mind and spirit. The second hour focuses on your physical condition. The two hours work hand-in-hand and enhance each other. Remember, your brain depends upon your body for nutrients, oxygen, water, and everything else needed to keep it in top form. While the human body is resilient, and there are some cases, such as the great scientist Stephen Hawking, where the body was severely diseased but the brain still operated at a high level, those are the exceptions. For most people, the functioning of the brain is closely related to the overall health of the body.

Here's the daily exercise schedule that we recommend. Please be advised that you should do the fitness routine that works for you. If you have any concerns about an exercise regimen, please consult your doctor.

45 minutes: Aerobic exercise, four days a week.

15 minutes: Core exercise, four days a week.

30 minutes: Weight training, two days a week.

One day of rest.

This can be adjusted, but most importantly it's a minimum of four to five hours per week of vigorous exercise each morning.

When you think "Daily Strength Builder" it's exactly what it states. It's a "daily process building" your strength. If you're new to the strength process start slowly and build up daily, like building blocks. Your daily workouts combined with your mind body development is another part of your journey to becoming invaluable.

In fact, physical fitness trainers recognize at least seven different types of muscular strength, each with its own advantages and limitations. You may have one type and not another, and each one represents a different path to becoming invaluable. They're differentiated in part by two different kinds of muscle fibers in your body.

"Fast-twitch" muscle fibers support quick, powerful movements such as sprinting or weightlifting. However, these relatively large fibers are quicker to fatigue.

"Slow-twitch" muscle fibers support long-distance endurance activities like marathon running. Although smaller than fast-twitch fibers, they are surrounded by more capillaries, which supports aerobic metabolism and fatigue resistance, particularly important for prolonged submaximal (aerobic) exercise activities.

While all of your muscles are a mix of fast-twitch and slow-twitch fibers, power athletes have a higher ratio of fast-twitch fibers, whereas endurance athletes have relatively more slow-twitch fibers.

Aerobic Exercise

By definition, "aerobic" exercise means "with oxygen." Typically, when referring to aerobic exercise we mean activities like running, jumping, swimming, cycling, basketball, tennis, or soccer. During aerobic activity, you repeatedly engage the large muscles in your arms, legs, and hips. For fuel, your muscles burn oxygen and glucose and then fat. The supply of oxygen must be quickly replenished, so when you exercise you breathe faster and more deeply, maximizing the amount of oxygen in your blood. Your heart will beat faster, increasing the flow of oxygen-rich blood to your muscles, where it picks up carbon dioxide and returns to your lungs.

Your body will also release endorphins, natural painkillers that promote an increased sense of well-being.

Here are ten ways, suggested by the Mayo Clinic, that aerobic activity can help you function at your highest level and become invaluable.

1. Increase your fitness, stamina, and strength. When you first begin regular aerobic exercise, you may quickly feel tired. But over the long term you'll experience increased stamina and reduced fatigue. You can also gain increased heart and lung fitness as well as bone and muscle strength.

2. Strengthen your heart. As the center of your cardiovascular system, your heart is key to nearly everything that gives your body life, from the transportation of oxygen to the effectiveness of your immune system. A stronger heart pumps blood more efficiently, which improves the flow of oxygen and glucose to all parts of your body.

3. Keep off the excess pounds. Combined with a healthy diet, aerobic exercise helps you lose weight and keep it off. While the number of calories you will burn in forty-five minutes of exercise depends on the type of activity you do and its intensity, the average person can burn up to four hundred calories in one session.

4. Ward off viral illnesses. Aerobic exercise strengthens your immune system, leaving you less susceptible to viral illnesses, including colds and the flu. Evidence suggests rigorous physical activity may help flush bacteria out of the lungs and airways, thereby reducing your chance of getting a cold, flu, or other illness.

5. Keep your arteries open. Aerobic exercise boosts your high-density lipoprotein (HDL), the "good" cholesterol, while lowering your low-density lipoprotein (LDL), the "bad" cholesterol. This may result in less buildup of plaques in your arteries.

6. Boost your mood. Physical activity may help boost production of endorphins, your brain's feel-good neurotransmitters. Although this function is often referred to as a "runner's high," any aerobic activity, such as a brisk game of tennis or a nature hike, can contribute to this same feeling. Numerous studies have shown that aerobic exercise can have meaningful reductions in symptoms of depression and improve cardiorespiratory fitness in people with major depressive disorder.

7. Reduce your overall health risks. Aerobic exercise reduces your risk of many conditions including high blood pressure, type 2 diabetes, metabolic syndrome, obesity, heart disease, stroke, and certain types of cancer. Weight-bearing aerobic exercises, such as jogging, help lower the risk of osteoporosis and lower your blood pressure. It can reduce the sensation of pain and improve function in people with arthritis. It can also improve the quality of life and fitness in people who've had cancer. If you have coronary artery disease, aerobic exercise may help you manage your condition.

8. Stay active and independent as you age. By keeping your muscles strong, aerobic exercise can help you maintain mobility as you get older. It can also lower the risk of falling and being injured from falls in older adults.

Because of its infusion of oxygen into your bloodstream, aerobic exercise helps keep your mind sharp and protects your memory, reasoning, judgment, and thinking skills (cognitive function), especially in older adults. It can even help delay the onset of dementia and improve cognition in people with dementia.

9. Help you look better! People who engage in aerobic exercise—even just a brisk walk every day—have that unmistakable healthy glow and better posture than those who are sedentary. Their eyes sparkle, and they often have a ready smile because they feel good inside.

10. Live longer. This is the bottom line, isn't it? Studies show that people who engage in regular aerobic exercise live longer than those who don't, and they have a lower risk of dying of all causes, including heart disease and certain cancers.[35]

Bonus benefit: Exercise in the morning may help you get better sleep that night! Elevating your metabolic rate with vigorous morning aerobics creates a hormonal balance and delivers a good night's sleep. According to a study published in *Vascular Health and Risk Management,* adults received better sleep on days they exercised around 7:00 AM. Participants spent more time in deep sleep after the morning workout and had fewer midnight awakenings.[36]

---

35 https://www.mayoclinic.org/healthy-lifestyle/fitness/in-depth/aerobic-exercise/art-20045541

36 https://blog.decathlon.in/articles/20-morning-exercises-that-you-can-do-at-home

So how can you do an aerobic exercise in the morning at home without driving to the gym?

To get forty-five minutes of aerobic exercise at home, the easiest thing to do is get out and walk vigorously or run around your neighborhood. You can establish a route by simply walking, jogging, running, or biking from your front door in any direction. Continue for twenty minutes. Then just turn around and retrace your steps. Voilà —you'll arrive home about forty-five minutes later, because you may be traveling a bit slower during the second half. You can also use a distance meter or app to chart a course that will take you forty-five minutes to complete.

If the weather is bad, you'll have to stay indoors. Our advice is to find an aerobic workout video—there are hundreds of them—and play it on your phone or laptop. Having an instructor act as a cheerleader can be very helpful!

You can also buy a stationary bike or treadmill that comes with a subscription to an online exercise program. This is the business model of Peloton, Life Fitness, SoulCycle, NordicTrack, Bowflex, and other companies. The concept is aimed toward people who may not have the opportunity to attend gym fitness classes or find a home-based class to be more convenient.

Core Exercise

In addition to forty-five minutes of aerobic exercise, four days a week, you should complete fifteen minutes of core exercise four days a week.

What's core exercise?

Your core refers to the muscles of your torso that provide both motion and stability for your spine and trunk. They aid in balance and postural support and help produce sport-specific movements to generate torque and force. It's important for everyone, and even more so as people age, because these muscles help keep you stable and prevent falls and injury. A strong core makes it possible for an elderly person to run their own errands, put away their own groceries, and play with the grandkids. You could say it represents the difference between truly living in old age rather than simply surviving. Because the core is a key part of the torso that keeps you together, it should be working for you all day long—and for your entire life.

As Harvard Health points out, your core muscles are important not just for athletics but for a multitude of routine tasks and activities:

Everyday actions. Sitting upright in a chair, bathing, dressing, bending to put on shoes or pick up a package, or turning to look behind you are just a few of the countless mundane actions that rely on your core and that you don't notice until they become difficult or painful.

Housework and gardening. Any kind of bending, carrying, hammering, lifting, twisting, and reaching overhead are acts that utilize core muscles. Simple chores like weeding the garden, vacuuming, mopping, and dusting become difficult if your core—particularly your back muscles—are sore or damaged.

Workplace tasks. Jobs that involve lifting, twisting, and standing all rely on core muscles. But less obvious tasks including making phone calls, typing, or using the computer can make back muscles surprisingly stiff and sore if you're not strong enough to practice good posture.

Sports and other recreational activities. Golfing, swimming, biking, tennis or other racquet sports, volleyball, running, baseball, rowing, kayaking, and many other athletic activities are supported by a strong core. And let's not forget sexual activities, which also call for core power and flexibility.

Balance while moving. Your core supports and stabilizes your body, allowing you to walk or run in any direction, even on rugged terrain, without losing your balance.

Making a good impression. Did you ever notice how successful politicians and other leaders have good, upright posture that signifies confidence? Weak core muscles contribute to slouching, while strong muscles enhance your silhouette and project authority. Core fitness lessens wear and tear on the spine and allows you to breathe deeply.

Avoiding back pain. Lower back pain—a debilitating, sometimes excruciating condition affecting four out of five Americans at some point in their lives—can often be prevented by well-balanced, resilient core muscles. For those afflicted with back pain, a regimen of core exercises is often prescribed to help relieve it.[37]

In just fifteen minutes, you're going to want to get a workout that impacts as many of these twenty-nine muscle pairs as possible. That's why it makes sense to focus on compound exercises, which work multiple muscle groups at the same time, rather than abs-focused exercises, such as sit-ups, which target a narrow group. While developing your abs gives you that "six-pack" look, if you ignore the others you'll increase the risk of muscle imbalances. The muscles on the weaker side of the body can become more vulnerable to injury while training, while those on the stronger side can suffer an overuse injury.

It's important to first develop strength in your deep abdominal muscles before moving onto your superficial core muscles. With strong deep abdominal muscles, your core is more likely to engage and work effectively in compound exercises.

---

37 https://www.health.harvard.edu/healthbeat/the-real-world-benefits-of-strengthening-your-core

During most exercises, you'll train and strengthen your core, but there are several core muscle-specific exercises worth incorporating into your core fitness routine. If you're a beginner and need guidance, a good place to start is the internet. If you google "core strength exercises," you'll find dozens of free videos with varying lengths and degrees of difficulty. An advantage of videos is that they have an instructor who leads you through the workout so you stay on track and on time. One of our favorites is "The New York Times Standing 7-Minute Workout," which is very convenient because it requires no equipment other than a wall and a chair, and you don't even need to get down on the floor. You can vary the exercises according to your level of fitness. If you do it twice, there's your fifteen minutes. You can also find many fifteen-minute low-impact core workout videos that you can do at home with no special equipment. Many of these videos focus on your six-pack because that's what sells, so be sure to get a good all-round core workout. If you have gym or exercise gear at home, then you can incorporate it into your routine.

Depending on your level of fitness, there are endless combinations and degrees of difficulty. Find a routine that works for you, and as you become more fit, try doing the same exercises while holding five or ten-pound weights in your hands. Remember, you're only spending fifteen minutes in this portion of the workout, so keep it simple so you can go quickly from one exercise to the next.

Weight Training

After your forty-five minutes of aerobic exercise, four days a week, and your fifteen minutes of core exercise, four days a week, then at least two days a week you should perform thirty minutes of weight training.

Weight training is any organized exercise in which muscles of the body are forced to contract under tension using external weights, body weight, or tension devices in order to stimulate growth, strength, power, and endurance. Weight training is also called "resistance training" and "strength training."

Why only two days a week and not four or five? Because unlike aerobic and core training, weight training to increase and strengthen muscles requires a substantial period of rest between sessions. This is necessary because resistance training causes trauma or injury of the cellular proteins in muscle. This prompts cell-signaling messages to activate satellite cells to begin a cascade of events leading to muscle repair and growth. The adaptation of muscle to the overload stress of resistance exercise begins immediately after each exercise session but takes time to physically manifest itself. It's the healing of those tiny tears that make your muscles grow in size and strength. In a sense, your muscles naturally "build back better." But if you keep training hard without rest days, you could defeat those gains and break your body down more than you build it up. The most adaptable tissue in the human body is skeletal muscle, and it is naturally remodeled during a carefully designed resistance exercise training programs, but only as long as sufficient time to rebuild is allowed.[38]

Overtraining can lead to injury. It's simple math. Traumatize your muscles too much, and those microtears will blossom into an injury that will lead to pain and set you back in your training.

But literally resting—like sitting on the sofa staring and at the TV—is not what you want either. (It's *never* what you want!) You should keep moving enough to increase blood flow to your muscles, which helps with the healing process. Your

---

38 http://www.unm.edu/~lkravitz/Article%20folder/musclesgrowLK.html

aerobics and core training are good to continue because you're not putting much strain on the muscles targeted in weight training. Remember, moving vigorously is *always* good. It's what your body was designed to do.

You'll know you're due for a break from weight training—or any intensive workout—if you're constantly sore, aren't making progress, feel like you're actually getting weaker, or are just bored or burned out. But normally, a two to three-day chill period is enough to get recharged and your muscles repaired. The time off will help you come back stronger and more motivated than before.

You can also invest in countless other devices for weight training, core training, and aerobics. Some are just old-fashioned analog machines, while many others are internet connected and offer guided workouts by professional trainers. If you want, you can pedal your Peloton stationary bike and look at the screen and imagine you're biking on a country road in Italy or across the Painted Desert in Utah!

The key to success at weight training is to *do what works for you*. You don't have to look like a body builder with bulging muscles. In fact, it's worth thinking about the method followed by legendary football quarterback Tom Brady—certainly an invaluable player if there ever was one! Unlike other NFL players who are known for size and strength, Brady follows a fitness regimen that focuses on *muscular pliability*. His TB12 Method of pliability is a combination of muscle strength, endurance, and most importantly flexibility. Muscular flexibility is defined as the ability to move a certain joint of the body through its entire range of motion without limitation. Developing flexibility in all of the muscle groups throughout the body allows you to perform tasks without tightness or stiffness, and decreases the odds of incurring a musculoskeletal injury such as a muscle strain—especially if a three-hundred-pound defensive lineman slams into you. In various interviews, Brady has explained that pliability is his attempt to keep his muscles "soft, long, and ready to move."

The important part of pliability is controlled stretching of the joints and muscles. There are two ways to do this.

Dynamic means controlled and active movement of part of your body through its available range, either at an increasing speed or increasing movement of body part. This is often done as a warm-up prior to a workout or athletic activity.

Static means moving a part of your body to the end of its available range of motion and holding that position for a defined length of time. This is done to improve range of motion.

As we age, pliability and muscular flexibility are the keys to strength and endurance, leading to a healthy, active, and pain-free life. As Tom Brady said, "It's not one thing, it's everything."[39]

As for weight training, instead of physical weights Brady uses elastic resistance bands. After a warmup, he completes nine moves: standing row, banded pushup, banded core rotations, deadlift, bicep curl, banded tricep extension, deceleration lunges, banded shoulder press, and X-band squat. With this routine, Brady hits multiple muscle groups and gets a full-body workout. And he doesn't count reps or sets! He just goes until the muscle fails. Then he moves to the next exercise. His focus is always on *proper form*. As he told *Health Digest*, if he falls out of form, then "other muscles are compensating for the muscle that should be working, and unless I stop, my brain will learn a new behavior—in this case, a negative one. Athletes often say, 'I did ten reps!' But what if after the fourth or

---

39 https://ptsmc.com/tom-brady-pliability#:~:text=In%20various%20interviews%2C%20he's%20explained,able%20to%20accept%20those%20demands.

fifth rep, their form begins breaking down?" If that happens, injury could follow.[40]

Here's one more tip from Brady. Get plenty of sleep. He's usually in bed at 9:00 PM and up at 6:00 AM. That's a solid nine hours! And before bed he avoids exercise, food, alcohol, caffeine, and electronics—all of which can disturb your sleep.

No matter how you do it, the benefits of weight training are significant:

Develop strong bones. By stressing your bones, strength training increases bone density and reduces the risk of osteoporosis. This is particularly important because as you age, without resistance training or vigorous physical activity your bones will gradually lose mass and become more brittle. Numerous studies have shown that strength training can slow bone loss, and several show it can even build bone, even among elderly people. Strength training in particular targets bones of the hips, spine, and wrists, which are the sites most likely to fracture.

Manage chronic conditions. Strength training has been shown to alleviate the signs and symptoms of many chronic conditions including arthritis, depression, obesity, back pain, heart disease, and diabetes.

Sharpen your mental acuity. Some research suggests that regular strength training and aerobic exercise improves cognitive skills for older adults.

Manage your weight. While strength training alone is not a weight loss strategy (by volume, muscle weighs much more than fat because it's more dense), in conjunction with proper diet and exercise it can increase your metabolism to help you burn more calories while helping you lose weight.

40 Health Digest. https://www.healthdigest.com/323870/tom-bradys-intense-routine-that-keeps-him-so-fit/

Enhance your quality of life. Strength training may protect your joints from injury, reduce your risk of falls, improve your ability to do everyday activities, and enhance your quality of life. All of these benefits can help you maintain independence as you age.

To become invaluable to your family and your community—and to live a longer and healthier life—you owe it to yourself to maintain a regular schedule of aerobic exercise, core exercise, and weight training. You'll be glad you did—not only today but as you grow older and find that you're still mentally sharp and physically strong.

You might find inspiration from Jim Arrington, who at the age of ninety was still regularly weight training. He started when he was fourteen, and although he won some competitions but never became a champion bodybuilder because he didn't have the right physique, he stuck with it for the next seventy-five years. In 2018, the *Guinness Book of World Records* anointed him "Oldest Male Bodybuilder."

In 2022, he told *Men's Health* magazine, "I train at the Mecca of bodybuilding, at Gold's Gym in Venice. I see a lot of bodies—if I compare myself to them, I'm nothing. But those people respect me for being what I am at the age I am. Training feels great. I get a little pump in, and there's people at the gym—you don't have long conversations with them, but they know you and they respect you because you're in there every day."[41]

As the classic Aretha Franklin song says, "R-E-S-P-E-C-T: Find out what it means to me!" It can mean a lot!

---

41 Men's Health. https://www.menshealth.com/fitness/a40983090/every-body-is-perfect-jim-arrington/

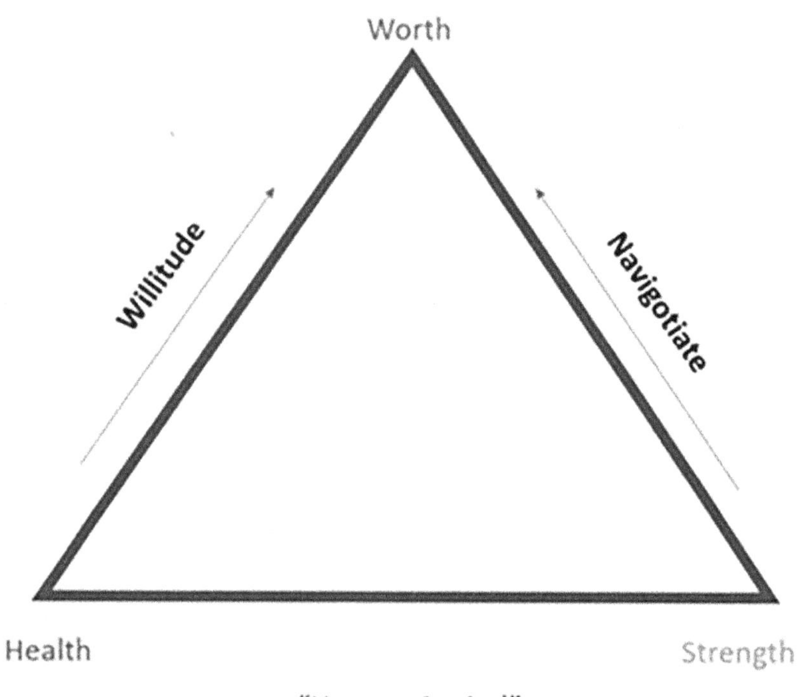
Worth
Willitude
Navigotiate
Health
Strength
"Human Capital"

Invaluable Spotlight Profile: Jason Johnson

Jason Johnson is the co-founder and CEO of Exclusive Charter Service, also known as ECS Jets, which provides 24/7 global aircraft charters.

His dad was the type of guy who would give you his shirt off his back, even if he had no other shirt. He taught Jason integrity and honesty. His great grandfather gave him good advice too: "Honor your mother and father, because one day you'll be a father," and "Always think in a straight line."

Jason started his career in business aviation at the early age of fifteen, working for New York Jet as a technician servicing general aviation and business jets. In 2004, he and his partner, Adam Klein, started ECS Jets as a charter brokerage, and then they grew their business. Unfortunately, in 2018 Adam died of cancer at the age of forty-two—a huge loss and a business challenge for Jason. But failure was not an option.

He and his company became invaluable by paying attention to the smallest details. For example, he went to Bed, Bath & Beyond and bought inexpensive towels with initials already embroidered on them. For every flight, they would put the towel in the bathroom with the correct initial of the client. This small investment yielded him some of the best repeat customers.

Jason believes there are two types of people. The first are those who have long-term values and vision, and the second are those who just want to make the quick buck. He likes to think of himself as the dumbest guy in the room who's always ready to learn from others.

THE BOTTOM LINE!

- Your Daily Strength Builder plan needs to be done according to a steady, disciplined schedule.
- Your first two hours set the stage to help make it a great day—and then a great week, month, and year. You use those two hours for mental and physical fitness, planning, and daily action.
- Hour one: Prepare your mind and spirit with meditation, goal setting and review, reading, and spiritual contemplation.
- Hour two: Prepare your body with exercise—aerobic, core, and strength training.

SELF-WORTH

At the very top of our Invaluable Pyramid is self-worth. When you reach the top, you have a positive feeling about yourself and see yourself as invaluable to others—not in an egotistical way but as a servant leader, which we discussed earlier in this book. Your willitude and your ability to navigotiate are highly developed, and your health and strength combine to form a strong source of human capital.

Self-worth is nominally intangible—it doesn't have physical size or weight, like your body does. It's not the size of your bank account or how many cars or houses you own. But it can be perceived, both by you and people around you. It's expressed to others by how you act, how you speak, and the choices you make. It's expressed by how productive you are versus how much you consume.

Before we continue talking about high self-worth, let's discuss its undesirable opposite, low self-worth.

The Warning Signs of Low Self-Worth

Low self-worth is having a generally negative overall opinion of oneself, placing a general negative value on oneself as a person and judging or evaluating oneself critically. People with low self-worth often focus on their mistakes (even trivial ones), what they didn't accomplish, or what other people did that was hurtful. They criticize themselves and their abilities, reject compliments, and deny their positive qualities.

Low self-worth can spring from adverse childhood experiences, such as when a child is led to believe they are not good enough, pretty enough, or smart enough, and this negative narrative stays with them into adulthood. It can lead the child—now an adult—to seek out or even fabricate conditions that mimic their childhood and confirm to them what they've been taught about themselves is true.

When someone believes they are of little worth, even if they attempt to conceal their true feelings, they often send out signals to those around them that can be readily perceived.

These signals may manifest in different ways for people. For example, eating disorders are a sign of low self-worth. When someone suffers from anorexia nervosa, you can tell by their dramatic weight loss that something is wrong. If they have trichotillomania, they pull out their own hair, which should be evident to a parent or experienced teacher. Someone who drinks excessively or takes addictive drugs is signaling to those around them that they have a problem with their self-esteem. Brooding, self-isolation, and antisocial posts on social media can all be signs of low worth. Such individuals may benefit from an intervention from loved ones and professional mental health treatment.

We should not ignore the ultimate act of low self-worth—taking your own life. Some people reach the point in life where they're so troubled that they believe the only way to deal with the feeling is to step away from life and into the other realm. Sometimes there are warning signs, such as suicidal talk or an unsuccessful attempt at suicide. But often there are no clear signs. Statistically, women have a higher rate of diagnosis of depression than men and are more likely to attempt suicide. In the United States, for example, adult women have reported a suicide attempt 1.2 times as often as men. But men attempt *and complete* suicide roughly three times as often as women. You might conclude that when a woman tries to end her life it's a cry for help, but when men do it's a final statement.

A more subtle form of low self-worth is simply being a consumer far more than a producer. People who overeat while sitting and watching the TV and do as little productive work as possible are signaling they have a poor opinion of themselves. If you don't have a sense of self-worth and respect for yourself, then you can't give that to other people.

On the other side of the coin, people who get up, go to work, and are productive are more engaged with others and have a much more positive view of the world and themselves. They are much more likely to be invaluable to the people around them.

Self-Worth Is Self-Generated

Self-worth is not about the size of your bank account, your job title, or your membership in an exclusive golf club. It's how you perceive yourself. You get your self-worth perspective when you look in the mirror.

This is *internal inspiration*, which comes from deep within, versus *external motivation,* which comes from other people. When you consider self-worth, how you feel about yourself is the "inside-out look" versus the "outside-in look." Too many people run around worrying too much about what other people think of them. They tend to be focused more on what other people think rather than how they feel about themselves first. This ties back to health and strength, because if you have your health and are taking care of yourself, you feel better about yourself and have energy.

Here's a thought experiment. If the world were to turn upside down and you were left with nothing—no family, no money, no assets—what then would you be ultimately worth? What could you do to scratch your way back to something? Would you say, "You can knock me down, but I can stand back up again and again." Could you muster the self-worth to go boldly forward into the unknown?

It's about loving yourself and believing in yourself so much that it's all you really need. You are not dependent on another's opinion of you, only your opinion of yourself.

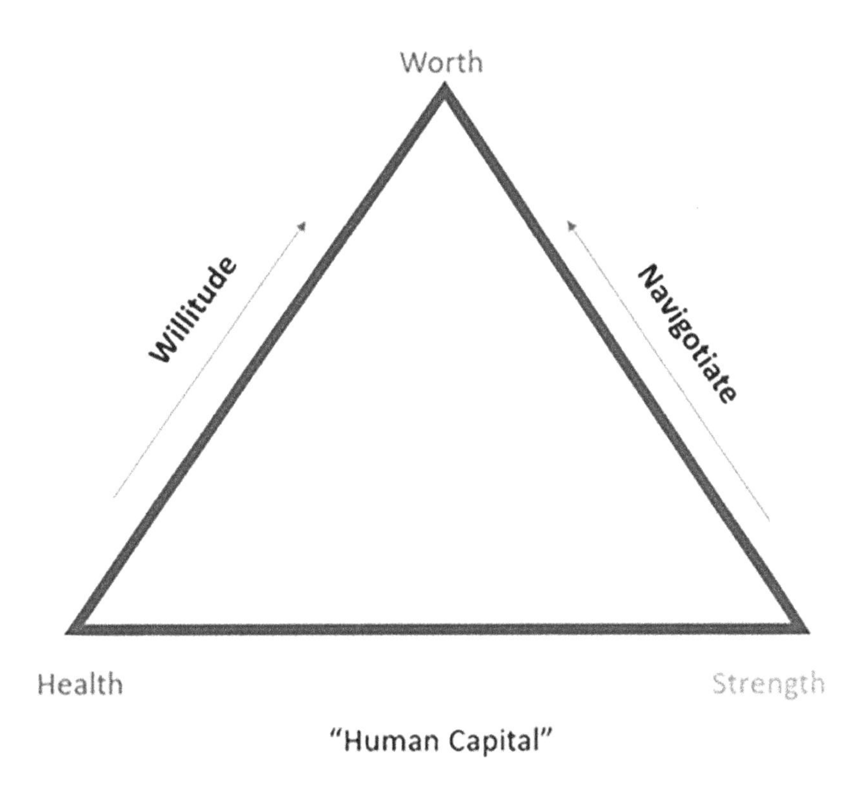

The foundation of our pyramid is strength and health as we know, and then we navigate through life building our value. By navigotiating and possessing the willitude to build our lives, we are creating our self-worth at the top of the pyramid. Worth is our return on investment, or ROI.

Hopefully everyone reading our book will invest in themselves and do what it takes to create a better wealth of worth for themselves, which means investing in ourselves mentally, emotionally, spiritually, physically, financially, in relationships, and occupationally.

You must feel good about yourself in whatever you do and how you operate. This ties right back to your purpose and values. How you feel about what you do relates to the purpose that you establish for yourself and consistently living by the values you have committed to uphold.

As we've seen, "What is my purpose?" is not always an easy question to answer. We ask ourselves, "Why do I exist? What inspires me about my existence in this world?"

Energy and emotion are connected as well. Some people blame others who look good or are achieving and put them down to feel better about themselves. The whole point is we all need to invest in ourselves first. What and how do you invest in yourself? How much time are you aware that you need to move, need to exercise, need to sleep, need to hydrate, need to eat, and need to rest? Everyone needs to have self-awareness of the key aspects that make them excellent.

Energy and emotion are like a fuel tank. When you expend energy and burn fuel to drive from point A to point B, you can't just keep driving forever; you need to refuel. You need to refuel yourself mentally and emotionally. That refueling factor is what we are stressing in self-worth. What do you put into yourself to be a better you?

You also don't have to just refuel. You need to maintain yourself as well. This is about preventative maintenance. Refueling and preventative maintenance are a daily activity necessary to have and keep a high sense of self-worth.

You can't build worth in others beyond what you have in yourself. You can only feed off what you have. You cannot teach someone something that you have not experienced yourself.

We all must invest in our development to enable ourselves to help develop others.

Project a Positive Self Image

One's sense of self-worth is often reflected in, and thereby visible to others, through body language, physical posture, and how you carry yourself. Self-worth can be observed. It's visible to other people when you have high self-worth and when you don't. You may not notice, and frankly others may or may not identify these reflections of self-worth consciously, but our subconscious minds are constantly observing.

We think we can approach people who'll help us develop more self-worth, more money, or more confidence, but in reality you have to do it yourself. Worth is first from inspiration with additional external influences that support our sense of self-worth.

The crap that happens to you either gets you sucked further down the toilet or can help you rise above it all. The inability to overcome obstacles will actually zap your self-worth. A common characteristic of low self-worth in people is they will be very critical of others and everything around them versus being complimentary about things around them. People who have a high self-worth of themselves tend to be very complimentary to others. If I'm good with me, then I'm not threatened by people around me and want to uplift you and others.

Twenty Life Hacks to Boost Your Self Worth

Here are twenty practical, everyday life hacks you can do to invest in your self worth.

1. Tell someone else how much you appreciate them. Being open and honest is important for self-worth, and the person receiving your appreciation will value you even more.
2. At the end of each day, before going to bed, write down something you feel proud about, either on that day or in the recent past. It need not be a big thing—remember, the little things add up to big results!
3. Say "no" to an unreasonable request. Learn the fine art of saying "no" without offending the person asking. You have the right to control your time and energy, and you shouldn't be "guilted" into doing something you don't want to do.
4. When you walk, do it tall and proud. Walk as if you've got somewhere to go and you need to be there. Never run! Just walk with deliberate intent and purpose. Radiate confidence and poise.
5. Do every task to the best of your ability. Even if it's just cleaning the bathroom or something equally as mundane, develop a reputation as someone who takes pride in their work.

6. Do something for yourself every day. Not something trivial or damaging, like eating an extra donut, but something that will make you smarter and more competitive.

7. Learn a new skill or take up something you've always wanted to do and stick with it. In particular, try something you've always assumed you couldn't do.

8. Dress to impress for each occasion, whether it be work, meeting a friend, or going for an interview. Do not be vain, but take pride in your appearance. It will put you into a winning frame of mind.

9. Read a book a month. In this media-driven, short-attention-span world, reading a real book is an achievement, and it's a great way to achieve a sense of accomplishment.

10. In every area of your life, speak up for yourself. Be polite but firm. This might be hard to do at first, but it will be empowering. If you maintain this, your feelings of self-worth will soar.

11. Listen to other people and what they are saying. Nothing makes another person feel valued more than being listened to. Listening does not equal endorsing or agreeing—you can listen while still holding onto your own beliefs. There is a difference between listening and just waiting for your turn to talk.

12. Stay away from people who are dragging you down. Let them live their lives and spin their webs of negativity, but don't get sucked into their dramas.

13. Work to maximize your strengths. Many people focus on trying to fix their weaknesses, but you'll get better results if you concentrate on what you are good at.

14. Stick to your core values. Don't succumb to pressure from social media or passing fads to do things that run counter to your values.

15. Reward your successes. As soon as you achieve something, step back and say to yourself, "Job well done!"

16. Forgive yourself! We all make mistakes. We're all human. When you mess up, make amends if required and then move on. The past is gone, and the future is what matters.

17. Get off social media for a week. Don't worry, you'll live! Then gauge how you feel about yourself and the world around you.

18. Stop gossiping! Don't go down into the gutter. Stay above it, and people will trust you.

19. Always be honest with yourself and others. Maintaining a falsehood will eat at your conscience, and the energy it takes to continue a lie is unsustainable.

20. Change your thinking to be more optimistic about yourself. Instead of saying, "I can't do that," say "I've never tried it, but I'll give it a shot!"

Invaluable Spotlight Profile: Jim Voss

Jim Voss is the CEO of Tenneco, one of the world's leading designers, manufacturers, and marketers of automotive products for original equipment and aftermarket customers, with approximately 71,000 team members working at more than two hundred sites worldwide.

Growing up, Jim always felt he was a little different from his friends. At a young age, he had a tremendous work ethic and a drive to succeed and make his own money. When he was twelve years old, he met the park director at the local pool and got hired, which meant he left the house on weekends at 5AM when it was still dark outside.

After high school, he eventually got a job at UPS loading trucks, which he loved. After completing his degree while working full time sixty to seventy hours a week, he decided to get his MBA. Doing it the way he did, he had a decade more years' work experience than all his colleagues.

For Jim, failure was never an option. He had a unique way of figuring out what he needed to do to win. "Don't wait for someone to train you," he says. "You need to find the right path to succeed or win. Great leaders don't look for blame, they look to see how they can muscle through it."

Invaluable people don't do things for themselves. They do things for other people. You're invaluable only if you feel that way!

THE BOTTOM LINE!

- At the very top of our Invaluable Pyramid is self-worth. It's the value you place on yourself. It's expressed to others by how you act, how you speak, the choices you make, and how productive you are versus how much you consume.
- You get your self-worth perspective when you look in the mirror or step back and see yourself objectively. This is *internal inspiration*, which comes from deep within, versus *external motivation*, which comes from other people.
- If the world were to turn upside down and you were left with nothing—no family, no money, no assets—what then would you be ultimately worth? What could you do to scratch your way back to something? Could you muster the self-worth to go boldly forward into the unknown?
- The chapter provides twenty life hacks that can boost your self-worth. Try to use one every day!

YOUR PERFORMANCE MINDSET

Do you want to know who you are? Don't ask. Act!
Action will delineate and define you.
– Thomas Jefferson

In order to be considered invaluable by your fellow human beings, you must provide verifiable evidence that you are, in fact, invaluable. It's a title you must earn through your deeds.

Thinking you're going to be invaluable some day in the future or that you were invaluable at some point in the distant past is not going to cut it.

Merely saying you are invaluable, without proof, does not meet the bar.

Hoping to become invaluable is nice, but it doesn't help anyone now.

To be truly invaluable, you need a performance mindset.

What does that mean?

A performance mindset is one in which your focus is to make a plan and then execute that plan, resulting in success.

Notice there are three words there: plan, execute, success. In that order.

To plan and execute to success requires knowledge, skills, and attitude, as well as good amounts of willitude and navigotiation. We also include the word "success" because you can have all the planning and execution you want, but if there's no success it won't matter and you will not be invaluable.

Think of a treasure hunter. Let's say the person believes a shipwreck loaded with gold lies off the coast of Florida. He raises money and plans the expedition to the last detail. He takes his boat out into the ocean and anchors over the site of the wreck. The professional divers go down to the wreck. They search it thoroughly. They find no gold. Nothing but sand. The expedition—well planned and properly executed—returns to port. The investors have lost their money. No one is invaluable!

For an individual (you), the performance mindset must include a multifaceted implementation plan that begins with self-development through health (mental and physical), strength (resiliency and stamina), and worth (your sense and understanding of self-worth and other-worth), combined with a daily, weekly, monthly, annual, and long-term implementation approach that separates you from the herd. This implementation plan should include your purpose, values, and vision, as well as your goals and objectives, all comprising your annual mission for action.

GOYA

There's an overall theme to this, which is: Get Off Your Ass, or GOYA. It's a simple slogan that was popularized by the 2019 book by Rick Thorn, Preston Thorn, and Wes Thorn entitled *G.O.Y.A.: Get Off Your Ass (G.O.Y.A. Introduction).*

Here's why it's important. You've got lots going on, and we'll bet you're often feeling deflated because you've got a list of things you must do but you can't fit them in. And you may be tempted to think, well, okay, I can't do that. I'll just skip it or put it off until next week.

The burdensome task could be a project at work or an obligation at home, such as to clean out the garage or fix a leaky faucet.

If you can reprogram your thinking with the concept of GOYA and very carefully schedule your time, you can get stuff done. What you want to do is right here, right now, and there can be no excuses.

Another example is your morning exercise routine. You remember:

- 45 minutes of aerobic exercise, four days a week.
- 15 minutes of core exercise, four days a week.
- 30 minutes of weight training, two days a week.

We're sure that fitness is really important to you, but when you're busy it can fall off your radar screen. Now thinking about GOYA, you might say, "I need to GOMA: Get Off My Ass and get my morning routine done. I'll get up one hour earlier every day (by being sure to go to bed one hour earlier every night) and make the routine happen."

Let's say you want to make a new landing page, implement a podcast, or a launch a new product for your business. You think, "I'm never going to get to this!" Rather than going home and flopping on the sofa with the TV remote, just spend ten, fifteen, or twenty minutes *every day* working on what's important. Put your plans into action, even if it's just baby steps. Before you know it, you'll achieve what you set out to do. You'll see why invaluable people implement GOYA even if they don't realize that's what they're doing.

The Movie in Your Head

It can be immensely valuable to envision, very clearly and realistically, your journey toward solving your problem or achieving your goal.

When planning a project and moving into your performance mindset, assume the role of a film director and make your movie. You start with the script. You are the star or hero of the movie, and you will overcome various obstacles to reach your goal and become invaluable.

Your movie can be very short—perhaps only a few scenes or even just one scene, anything that you can visualize in your mind. Another version of the movie in your head are the "vision boards" people put on the walls of their offices or homes. The vision board is a visual representation, in pictures, of your desired future state. It could be anything—a photo of yourself on the cover of *Time* magazine, a facsimile of a check for a million dollars, or a picture of a big corner office or a mansion on a hill. Your vision board is like the movie in your head, only it's a real picture on your wall.

Here's an example of the movie in your head or the vision board on your wall. Let's say you have obtained your license to be a real estate broker. This is your chosen career. Your goal is to be the top-rated, invaluable broker in your town. By the end of ten years, you want to be earning a personal income of at least $200,000 a year from your real estate business, as well as owning income-generating properties such as apartment buildings. Your ultimate goal at the end of 20 years is to be the number one owner of multi-family buildings in your town and enjoy a massive flow of passive income with a million dollars in the bank.

Envision the attributes you need to take to reach your goal. Let's break them down:

Knowledge. You need to become the expert in real estate in your town. You see yourself learning the history of the best properties, how much they're worth, and the sales trends. You know the top real estate attorneys, appraisers, and loan officers. You even know all the probate attorneys who can let you know when someone dies and their estate wants to quickly sell the house, and you know which houses are headed toward a foreclosure sale. You know the law, the intricacies of real estate financing, and the difference between a balloon payment and a payoff amount.

Skills. You can size up a house and determine its likely selling price. You can spot houses that have problems such as cracked foundations, termites, or mold. You know how to stage a house for the best price and how to negotiate with sellers and buyers alike. You have developed your listening and questioning skills in ways that you can gain the best understanding of what a buyer wants and help them achieve it, navigotiating the buyer and seller to closing the deal better and faster than anyone else in town. When you see a house that's run-down and shabby, you're the only agent in town who can see it restored and doubled in value. All of these things and more you can visualize in your mind's eye, just like a movie.

Attitude. You have a winning attitude. No one will serve their clients better than you. You show up on time and ready to make a deal. When one sale falls through, you brush it off and go to the next one. At the same time, you don't allow yourself to get bogged down by people who are just lookers and not buyers. You're good at qualifying clients and going after the ones who are serious—both sellers and buyers.

Willitude. You need to have the *willpower* and the *fortitude* to persevere during economic challenges. The real estate market can be volatile, and you need to be able to weather its ups and downs. It's also insanely competitive, because anybody can get a broker's license and call themselves a real estate agent. Only the strong survive!

Navigotiate. In every industry, the combination of *navigate* and *negotiate* is so important! It's important for criminal defense lawyers who must guide their clients through the justice system. It's important for supply chain managers signing contracts with foreign manufacturers, for Hollywood studio moguls to make deals to get a movie made, and for real estate agents seeking the best financing for their client. It's also important for the parent of a teenager who now has a mind of her own and can no longer be ordered around like when she was five.

All of these attributes are the tools that you can use to write the movie in your head that represents your performance mindset and documents your journey to becoming invaluable.

Seize the Opportunity!

The movie in your head is a form of the law of attraction. It's value is what it does to your expectations and your self-confidence. If you *see yourself* as a winner, you're far more likely to do what it takes to *be* a winner. In contrast, if you see yourself as a loser or a victim, you will not recognize or seize upon opportunities that come your way. If you get a good job, you won't hold onto it. If you can get drunk on a work night, forcing you to go to work late the next morning, you'll do that because you'll believe that's what you deserve. You'll say, "The other guy gets all the breaks. I never get a break." No, that's probably not true. You probably get the same number of "unearned" lucky breaks as the other person, but the difference is that he or she seizes upon them eagerly while you just shrug and let them pass by.

Here's an example. John and Sally are mid-level executives who both attend a local Chamber of Commerce breakfast meeting. As everyone knows, the point of these meetings is to "schmooze" with other businesspeople. At the meeting, John is introduced to Mike Smith, the CEO of First Bank, a local regional bank. John thinks nothing of it and after politely shaking hands with Mike drifts away into the crowd.

Sally is standing there too. She's introduced to Mike Smith. They shake hands.

Sally thinks to herself, "Wow! I'm meeting the CEO of First Bank! This is fantastic! I must get to know him."

Sally engages Mike in small talk and finds an area of common interest—say, a new park that's being built in town or the effort to clean up pollution in the river. No pressure, just a pleasant conversation. It lasts for a few minutes. Perhaps Sally finds a reason to give Mike her business card. They shake hands again and go their separate ways.

So what's the big deal? It was a brief conversation, but it was long enough that Mike formed a favorable impression of Sally and will remember her the next time they meet. As for John? Mike has little memory of him.

Again, what's the big deal? The big deal is that Sally does this *everywhere she goes*. She wants to know *everybody*. These short encounters, repeated over and over again, slowly build into a big pyramid of worth. They add to Sally's aura of invaluableness. They make her a known figure all over town and give her opportunities to demonstrate her knowledge, skills, and positive attitude. Doors will open for her. People will return her phone calls. And Mike, at the bank, might fast-track her business loan application.

Meanwhile, John, who does not think of himself as invaluable and does not recognize opportunities when he meets them, languishes in his job, unfulfilled and bored.

Don't be like John! Be like Sally. Get up in the morning with optimism, and as you complete your daily health and strength building routine review the movie in your head, look at your vision board, or make your list of "To Dos." Be in a performance mindset. Have a plan and follow it. Look for opportunities to fulfill your mission. Be grateful that such opportunities are presented to you. Value them and profit from them. That's how you make yourself invaluable.

Up, Relaxed, and Yes

While we're on the subject of meeting people and interacting with them in real life, author and body language expert Ken Delmar provides an effective tutorial in his book, *Winning Moves: Body Language for Business.* Written originally for salespeople, he reveals the secrets of how to make a positive impression through your body language, and how the wrong body language can convey a negative impression. He recommends these three steps: up, relaxed, and yes, or URY.

Up means you carry yourself with confidence and optimism. You radiate a positive vibe. When you present yourself, you're dressed appropriately and without needless distractions. Your job is to make the other person feel comfortable.

Relaxed means that no matter how high the stakes, you exude quiet authority. Nothing rattles you. When people are looking for a leader and someone who's invaluable, they don't want a person who is tense or preoccupied with some other matter. They want someone who is confident of a positive outcome for everyone.

Yes means you're focused on your performance mindset. You always want to avoid saying "no" and find a way to say "yes." For example, when your counterpart says, "Can you deliver the order by tomorrow," instead of saying no, you say, "To ensure the highest quality, we are happy to promise delivery in forty-eight hours." Always go for the "yes!"

In summary, when you say it out loud, "URY" means "You Are Why" positive outcomes occur wherever you are! Ken Delmar goes on to say that you should find that moment when you were at your best in life, one or two different thirty-second videos in your mind, and then before walking into a situation where you know you must perform at your very best—a sales call, presentation, musical performance, whatever it may be—take a moment to play this video to help remind yourself "URY!"[42]

This video, from Steve's personal experience, is *YOUR* video, not to be shared with others. Why? Because they may say something like, that was your best! Now the movie is less impactful or ruined. Keep it to yourself! It only matters what you think and feel from these videos in your mind. These thirty seconds may be from a sports event or a professional situation where you know you were at your absolute best! Steve still uses one from his high school basketball days. It helps put him in the performance zone for whatever sport he may be playing and has several others he uses for different situations.

---

42 https://www.amazon.com/Winning-Moves-Body-Language-Business/dp/1734488506/ref=tmm_pap_swatch_0?_encoding=UTF8&qid=1680796082&sr=1-1

Resiliency

No one's path to becoming invaluable is a straight line of successes. Everyone suffers setbacks. It is these challenges—and how you respond to them—that determine whether you will reach your goal.

Steve Jobs, the founder of Apple, is a favorite subject of business and self-help books for a very good reason. His short life was full of drama, highs and lows, and controversy and achievement. One thing is certain about him. He had resilience.

Jobs and his friend Steve Wozniak founded their little computer company in 1976 in the garage of Jobs's parents' house in Los Altos, California. By 1985, Apple was generating about $10 billion a year in revenues, but the company was in turmoil. Two years earlier, Jobs had brought in John Sculley to serve as CEO, and soon the two were clashing over company strategy. Sculley successfully exiled Jobs by making him head of new product development. Jobs then tried to get rid of Sculley, but the plan backfired, and Jobs resigned from the company he had founded. Apple's fortunes began to sink while Jobs founded a new computer company, NeXT, and then he co-founded the animated movie studio Pixar, its first film being the box office smash *Toy Story*.

In early 1997, with revenue dropping, Apple brought Jobs back, eventually naming him CEO. Reportedly, the company was virtually insolvent. Sales were dismal, and the product line was complicated. To satisfy requests from retailers, Apple had been making multiple versions of products, including twelve versions of the Macintosh computer.

After weeks of meeting with product people, Jobs had heard enough. According to Walter Isaacson in the book *Steve Jobs*, in the middle of a product meeting, Jobs shouted, "Stop! This is crazy!" He then announced the company would make just four basic computer models: home and office versions of the desktop and portable units. Seventy percent of the company's products were discontinued. From that day on, Apple began growing again, and the company never looked back.

That's resiliency, proof that at that time in history Steve Jobs was absolutely invaluable to the company.

When Jobs died of pancreatic cancer in 2011, many analysts thought that without him Apple would wither and decline. His successor, Tim Cook, a mild-mannered, nondescript man who had joined Apple in 1998, seemed to be as expendable as Jobs was invaluable. But as it turned out, Jobs had built a sturdy company, and since Cook assumed leadership in his low-key style, he has guided the company to stunning levels of success and profitability. It just goes to show you that there are many ways to be invaluable, and the best way is *your* way!

Be Physically and Mentally Agile

Earlier in the book, we discussed the importance of health and strength in your drive to become invaluable. To that we'd like to add physical and mental agility. They may seem to be two separate skills, but in reality they are closely connected and interdependent.

In business as in life, your physical agility conveys an impression to those around you. To illustrate this, consider these two scenarios.

Bob has been called up to make a presentation on a controversial topic. As he approaches the podium, he moves stiffly. Perhaps his breathing is labored as he walks slowly. When climbing the two or three steps to the stage he must hold the handrail and pull himself up. At the podium, he pauses to catch his breath and shuffle his papers. When he speaks, his presentation is halting, and he projects uncertainty. His audience may be empathetic and think, "Oh, poor Bob," but will they want to see him as an invaluable leader? Probably not!

Then it's Michelle's turn. With a light, confident step, she ascends the stairs, not bothering to hold the handrail. With a radiant smile, she looks out over the crowd. When she takes the microphone, she speaks clearly and with confidence. She has good posture and positive energy. When she speaks, she uses both hands to reinforce her point. When you watch her, you can't tell if she's left-handed or right-handed. In fact, while she's a pleasure to listen to, with a clear melodious voice, she's also a pleasure to watch. She commands your attention. Before you even consider the substance of what she's saying, she's got you on her side.

In how they respond to public figures and people who want to be leaders, audiences and the press can be either enthusiastic or merciless. Anyone who has watched candidates campaigning for high office knows that if a candidate stumbles while walking—even slightly—the video of the stumble will be replayed endlessly on TV and social media. The candidate's opponents will proclaim that the stumble proves the candidate is too old or too sick to serve and is unfit for office. Other gaffes—mispronounced words, lapses in memory—are also amplified and repeated.

In the old days, before the 24/7 news cycle, politicians and other leaders took great pains to hide their physical disabilities or challenges.

The most famous example is President Franklin D. Roosevelt. In 1921, when he was just thirty-nine years old, he was stricken with a crippling disease that was most likely polio. He nearly died, and when he recovered he had lost the use of his legs. Confined to a wheelchair, he could stand and walk only with the help of heavy steel leg braces. Despite this crippling handicap, he was twice elected governor of New York, in 1928 and again in 1930. Before he moved into the Governor's Mansion in Albany, the house was made wheelchair accessible with ramps and an elevator. In 1932, he won the presidential election in a landslide and became the first (and, as of 2023, only) physically disabled person to be president of the United States. Before he moved into the White House, ramps were discreetly added to make it wheelchair accessible.

In those days, it was much easier to shield a candidate or office holder from public scrutiny. Roosevelt's staff went to great lengths to hide his condition from the voters. The Secret

Service blocked photographers who tried to take pictures of the president in his wheelchair, even confiscating and destroying film. Roosevelt and his close confidants believed that especially during wartime, for Roosevelt to be an invaluable leader, he had to appear able-bodied. It was only at the very end of his career, on March 1, 1945, about a month before his death, that he said during his address to Congress, "I hope that you will pardon me for this unusual posture of sitting down, but I know you will realize that it makes it a lot easier for me not to have to carry about ten pounds of steel around on the bottom of my legs."[43]

President John F. Kennedy, who radiated an aura of youthful vitality, had a complex medical history that is now thought to be an autoimmune polyglandular syndrome type 2 with Addison's disease and hypothyroidism. From adolescence, he suffered with gastrointestinal symptoms, which now suggest coeliac disease. He was so ill at a few points during the 1950s that his Catholic priest administered last rites. He also had a chronic back problem, which contributed to a chronic pain syndrome. These problems began while playing football in college, and when he first volunteered for service in World War II his lower back pain was so severe he was initially rejected by both the US Army and the Navy. He underwent a total of four back operations, including a discectomy, an instrumentation, and fusion, and two relatively minor surgeries that failed to improve his pain. He wore a lumbar back brace right up until the moment of his tragic death on November 22, 1963. All of this was successfully hidden from the general public.

Times have changed. In 1984, at age twenty-six, Greg Abbott was paralyzed below the waist when an oak tree fell on him while he was jogging after a storm. Openly wheel-

43 FDR. "Address to Congress on Yalta (March 1, 1945)". Mar 1, 1945.

chair-bound, in 2002 he became attorney general of the state of Texas and was elected governor in 2014 then re-elected in 2018 and 2022. To his political followers, he exudes an air of authority and leadership, and the wheelchair doesn't matter.

In fact, with the right kind of attitude, having a disability can convey the impression that you are a fighter who will never give up. The voters will think, "Look at him! He's got guts to get up and assert himself."

Ultimately, your success depends on your mental attitude, strength, and agility.

The Agile Mind

Mental agility is the ability to think quickly on your feet. It means having a clear point of view and being able to defend it against attack, as well as remain open to even better ideas from others.

There are two kinds of mental agility, preparedness and quick response.

Preparedness. Let's say you're making a presentation to a skeptical business group—perhaps even your own colleagues and your boss. You have an idea or plan you'd like to propose. You know that for whatever reason—professional jealousy, fear of new ideas, a sincere desire to make your idea better, or whatever—some people will push back and offer criticism. Part of mental agility means being prepared *in advance* to respond to anticipated questions. Before you go up to the podium, you should have an answer for these negative comments:

"It will cost too much."

"We don't have the manpower."

"The technology is too advanced."

"It will drain other resources."

"It's just not something we can do."

And so on.

You need to think like a pro tennis player. You're on the court, and you know that when you hit the ball your opponent will swat it right back at you. That's just the way the game is played. You need to be prepared to drop back, rush the net, hit a backhand—whatever agile response is necessary to stay in the game. If you enter the game and unprepared for the expected responses, then it's your own fault if you get caught flat-footed.

Quick response. The other type of mental agility consists of your ability to quickly recognize and evaluate an unforeseen but potentially *helpful* comment or piece of information. So often we get caught up in our own brilliant idea that we feel as though *any* comment about it must be inherently negative, and so we're prepared to be defensive even before we've thought about the idea offered. Let's say you've proposed an idea for a new product, and Joe raises his hand and says, "Yes, this idea is a good one, but XYZ Company has a very similar product, and it might make more sense to work out a licensing agreement with them rather than spend the money developing it ourselves and perhaps get into a patent conflict with them."

The rigid mind will think, "No, no—this is my idea, and we're going to own it." In contrast, the agile mind will think, "Let's explore this new information. We may be in a good position to leverage existing technology for a low price."

We cannot begin to tell you how many capable companies and their leaders have been doomed by rigid, non-agile thinking. The agile mind is constantly collecting and reviewing new ideas, just like an innovation pipeline or funnel. All the new ideas—regardless of how crazy they may seem—enter the wide open end of the pipeline and move through it. As they travel, they're weeded out so that eventually only the good and useful ideas remain. This process must continue constantly in your mind and in your organization as a whole.

To understand how the human brain can reach its maximum agility and performance mindset, let's examine the physiology of the brain itself. Among its many other features, this incredibly complex machine is divided laterally into the right and left hemispheres. According to accepted science, each hemisphere has a different way of processing information. The left hemisphere generally controls language and motor abilities, whereas the right hemisphere is responsible for visual-spatial attention.

This matters because one side or the other almost always becomes dominant. Left-brain-dominant individuals tend to be objective and process information in a linear order. They process information in details and then put those details together as a whole. Left-brain thinkers are verbal and see things in an analytical or scientific way.

Right-brain-dominant people are visual and process the whole picture before seeing the details. These people are subjective and focus on aesthetics. They process information in a varied order and are typically creative in the way they think and more artistic in their abilities.

This division may be reflected in the fact that humans rarely use both hands equally, especially when doing such tasks as handwriting and eating. Although the percentage varies worldwide, in Western countries, up to ninety percent of people are right-handed and ten percent of people are left-handed. Mixed-handedness (preferring different hands for different tasks) and ambidextrousness (the ability to perform tasks equally well with either hand) are uncommon. This is one of the traits that separates us from most other primates, which don't often show any overall preference for left or right handedness.

The left and right hemispheres control motor action on the opposite sides of the body. So if you are a member of the right-handed majority, your left hemisphere is dominant. If you're one of the roughly ten percent of people who are left-handed, it's your right hemisphere that calls the shots.

The two hemispheres are linked by the corpus callosum. In terms of its shape, imagine a low, short bridge connecting two adjacent land areas. While a typical bridge would have two or four lanes of traffic, imagine this bridge has a million lanes of traffic going both ways. While it's large for a fiber tract, it's still tiny compared to the vast network of trillions of connections within each hemisphere. Physically, it is not feasible for the hemispheres to fully share information or to operate in a fully unified fashion. While the corpus callosum is a bridge, it's also a bottleneck.

Why is there a difference at all? Perhaps it's because while human society needs a vast number of practical, down-to-earth right-handers, it also needs a few people who are willing to think differently—that is, whose right hemisphere dominates. As the American Psychological Association noted, anecdotal evidence has traditionally suggested that lefties might think more creatively than right-handers, and research supports this notion. A 2007 paper in *Journal of Mental and Nervous Disease* found that musicians, painters, and writers were significantly more likely to be left-handed than control participants. While right-handers might dismiss an idea as too radical or unfamiliar, lefties might be willing to entertain the thought and develop a solution that a right-hander's brain would not have considered.[44]

---

44 Price, M. (2009, January 1). The left brain knows what the right hand is doing. Monitor on Psychology, 40(1). https://www.apa.org/monitor/2009/01/brain

But here's the really interesting thing. Despite the clear evidence that one hand dominates when performing everyday tasks, brain scans do not indicate any difference in brain activity. According to a 2013 study from the University of Utah, after looking at the brain scans of more than one thousand young people, no evidence of "sidedness" was found. The authors concluded that the notion of some people being more left-brained or right-brained is more a figure of speech than an anatomically accurate description.[45]

On the other hand, the claim that the left hemisphere is the seat of language comes from observations that damage to the left hemisphere (for example, due to a stroke) is often associated with difficulties producing language, a problem known as aphasia. As cognitive neuroscientist Kara D. Federmeier, a professor of psychology at the University of Illinois at Urbana-Champaign noted, for most people, the left hemisphere does play a much more important role in the ability to speak than the right hemisphere does. "Like other complex skills," she told NPR, "the ability to understand what we read or what someone is saying to us requires both hemispheres, working together and separately."[46]

Even with our advanced technology uncovering its secrets, the human brain remains an incredibly complex and mysterious machine!

To get back to the practical matter of becoming invaluable, whether you are right-handed or left-handed, the point is that you need to develop as much of your brainpower as possible.

---

45 Harvard Health. https://www.health.harvard.edu/blog/right-brainleft-brain-right-2017082512222

46 NPR. https://www.npr.org/sections/13.7/2013/12/02/248089436/the-truth-about-the-left-brain-right-brain-relationship

To do this, you need to understand the different types of brainwaves. These are oscillating electrical discharges produced by the roughly eighty-six billion neurons in the brain. Measuring just a few millionths of a volt, these discharges emanating from the neurons can be detected using a technique called electroencaphology, or EEG, in which sensors attached to the scalp detect those tiny bursts of energy and record them as waves. The frequency of the waves, from long to short, varies according to the activity of the brain at that moment.

There are five widely recognized brain waves, and each one is associated with a different state of mind. They are measured in hertz (Hz), the unit of frequency in the International System of Units, equivalent to one event or cycle per second. So, if a wave is 10 HZ, that means the crest-to-trough cycle happens ten times per second.

Delta Waves (.5-3 Hz)

Delta waves are the slowest frequency brain waves. They are associated with a state of deep, restful sleep and are thought to play a role in transferring learning and long-term memory storage. Delta waves can help improve your immune system and reduce stress levels, have been associated with a state of physical healing, and are thought to play a role in tissue repair and regeneration.

Theta Waves (4-7 Hz)

Theta waves are associated with a state of deep relaxation, light sleep, or drifting off to sleep. They are strong during internal focus, meditation, prayer, and spiritual awareness. They can help improve your mood and reduce stress levels, have been associated with a state of mental creativity, and are thought to play a role in imagination and intuition. Often seen in connection with creativity, intuition, daydreaming, and fantasizing, they are a repository for memories, emotions, and sensations.

Alpha Waves (8-12 Hz)

Alpha waves are associated with a state of relaxation, daydreaming, or meditating. They disappear when you're sleeping. Appearing to bridge the conscious to the subconscious, alpha waves can improve your ability to focus and concentrate and help to reduce stress and anxiety.

Alpha waves have been associated with a state of "mental readiness" and are thought to play a role in attention and focus. They may be considered a bridge from the external world to the internal world, and vice versa.

Beta Waves (14-38 Hz)

Beta waves are associated with a state of alertness, problem-solving, and mentally challenging tasks. Beta waves can help improve your memory and cognitive performance and are thought to play a role in concentration and focus. On the negative side, a flood of beta wave activity may produce a feeling of agitation.

Gamma Waves (30-80 Hz)

These high frequency waves are associated with concentrated information processing, high intelligence, and a feeling of happiness. When the brain needs to simultaneously process information from different areas, it's hypothesized that gamma activity consolidates the required areas for simultaneous processing. A good memory is associated with well-regulated and efficient gamma activity, whereas a gamma deficiency creates learning disabilities.

You can take steps to control your brainwave activity.

For example, regular meditation has been shown to increase alpha waves (your relaxation brain waves) while reducing beta waves (the brain waves of active thought and learning). This is useful for reducing stress. Techniques including closed-eye visualization and deep breathing, which are used in mindfulness meditation, also boost alpha waves. Alpha waves may also help boost creativity and promote the release of the neurotransmitter serotonin, which makes you feel happy.

You can also get into the "alpha flow" by doing any simple repetitive activity that does not require much focus or critical judgment, such as playing simple games, going for a run, washing dishes, or cleaning your house. When in flow, your brain is poised on the border between alpha and theta, around 8 Hz. You can lose your sense of time, your attention is consumed entirely, and your inner critic goes quiet.

Perhaps surprisingly, another way to boost your alpha waves is to do high-intensity workouts. Not only do they release endorphins that give that exercise "high," but they also promote alpha waves as you rest.

But if you want to increase your focus and attention, you should do the opposite: reduce your alpha waves. Studies have shown a decrease in alpha waves has been linked to enhanced attention. It's unclear if alpha waves control attention or are just a byproduct of some other process that governs attention.

Technology can help. Neurofeedback is a form of biofeedback, the mind-body technique designed to help the user gain voluntary control over certain body functions that are typically involuntary, such as heart rate, muscle contraction, or brainwaves. Neurofeedback teaches self-control of brain functions by measuring brain waves and providing a feedback signal. The user is connected to an electroencephalography (EEG) machine that analyzes brainwaves and displays them for the user, either in audio or video form. Positive or negative feedback is produced for desirable or undesirable brain activities, respectively. The user learns to recognize when their brain is in a certain state and can then consciously try to alter it. They can learn to recreate a desired state, such as relaxation, or avoid an undesired state, such as agitation, in their daily life.

When used clinically, a patient can learn to regulate and improve brain function and possibly alleviate symptoms of various neurological disorders and mental health conditions. Often used as a treatment for attention-deficit/hyperactivity disorder (ADHD), it's also been used to treat epilepsy, anxiety, depression, and insomnia.

The old saying "mind over matter" is really true! Your actions, how you appear to others, and your drive to become invaluable through your knowledge, skills, and attitude are all dependent on how you use your mind.

Invaluable Spotlight Profile: John Hardy

John Hardy founded Compass Moving and Storage in 2005 in Dennis, Massachusetts. He began with just one truck and a solid commitment to providing a professional, personal, and caring approach to moving. In the years since, he and his company have become invaluable to anyone moving to or from Cape Cod.

He enlisted in the Army when he was seventeen and served six years but was injured and given a medical discharge. He got married and bounced around, never finding his purpose until he went to Cape Cod to visit his grandfather. He liked the area, got into the moving business, and eventually started his own company. Today the business has twenty-two employees and eleven trucks as well as a profitable storage business.

What makes John invaluable to his family and community? If someone else says they can't do it, he says he can. He and his team always find a way to get something done, even if it's impossible for someone else. He says, "Never say, no, I can't do it.' Just find a way to do it. If someone else can do it, why can't I?"

Under pressure, John is very relaxed. His wife says his superpower is that when the world gets crazy everything seems to slow down for John.

He developed his willitude by saying, "Failure is not an option. Never give up. Create your own circumstance, always find a way to get it. You must be willing to help."

THE BOTTOM LINE!

- Your performance mindset comprises your focus to make a plan and then execute that plan, resulting in success. Notice the three words in this order: plan, execute, success.
- Get Off Your Ass, or GOYA, is a simple slogan that was popularized by the 2019 book by Rick Thorn, Preston Thorn, and Wes Thorn entitled *G.O.Y.A.: Get Off Your Ass (G.O.Y.A. Introduction)*. Reprogram your thinking with the concept of GOYA and very carefully schedule your time to get stuff done. There can be no excuses!
- Use the movie in your head. When planning a project and moving into your performance mindset, assume the role of a film director and make your movie. Envision the attributes you need to take to reach your goal. Its value is what it does to your expectations and your self-confidence. If you *see yourself* as a winner, you're far more likely to do what it takes to *be* a winner.
- Your success ultimately depends on your mental attitude, strength, and agility.
- You need to develop as much of your brainpower as possible. To do this, you need to understand the different types of brainwaves—delta, theta, alpha, beta, gamma.

FAILING FORWARD

Failure is the key to success.

What? Really? Could that be true?

Yes, because failure simply means that you took an action that produced a result that you did not think you wanted.

Does this mean the unwanted result has no value?

Absolutely not!

Every unwanted result has some value.

Let's take a look at the spectrum of failure to see why that's true.

Failure happens for two reasons.

1. You're not yet ready to succeed. By this we mean that the systems you have in place are not yet capable of producing success. For example, let's say you're a baby, less than one year old. You try to walk across the room and you fall flat on your face. Failure! Why did you fail? Not because you made a wrong choice. You failed because your muscles and brain had not yet learned how to master the complex activity of walking upright.

The solution is to keep trying! You don't have to "fix" anything in your approach. The unwanted result (falling) provided your developing brain with valuable information. The more you try to walk and then fall, the more your brain will learn, and you'll get better at it. Practice makes perfect.

This principle applies to businesses as well as individuals. For example, at the time of this writing, the massive Starship rocket, built by SpaceX, was sitting on the launch pad in South Texas with the launch delayed. The event was postponed because of technical issues. Was this a true "failure?" Of course not. The engineers decided the rocket—the world's most powerful—was not ready for flight.

2. You've made an incorrect choice. Life is full of decisions, and many of them will be wrong. You assemble the best information you have and go with it. There are always unknowns that appear later in the process. And sometimes you have many choices that all appear to be equivalent, so you just choose one and see what happens.

The most famous example of someone making repeated wrong choices and finally getting it right was when Thomas Edison and his team were trying to make a filament for their electric light bulb. The year was 1880. They knew the basics. They had the glass vacuum globe and the socket design, and they knew that they needed to pass an electric current through a thin filament to make it glow. The problem was the filaments they tested were either too expensive to be practical or burned out too quickly. So they methodically tried a succession of materials. Reportedly, they experimented with six thousand different materials until they tried carbonized cotton thread, which could burn for over fifteen hundred hours. Success! Interestingly, they had tried tungsten, which worked very well, but they considered it too difficult to work with. Twenty years later, an inventor named William David Coolidge invented the tungsten filament, which became the standard in every incandescent light bulb.

Of his search and repeated failures, Edison said, "I have not failed 10,000 times—I've successfully found 10,000 ways that will not work." When you think about it, that's quite true. When one choice results in failure, you can cross it off your list and try another solution.

Here's an incorrect choice that literally changed world history. In 1492, when Christopher Columbus set sail from Spain and headed west across the Atlantic Ocean, he thought he knew exactly where he was going, to what we now call the Pacific Rim region of China and Japan. The continent of Asia was well known to European traders, who traveled east to get there. But it was a long journey, and Columbus calculated he could travel the distance much more quickly by heading around the globe to the west. He was correct, except that he vastly underestimated the circumference of the earth. He had no idea that an entire continent lay in his path!

His mistake turned out to be something better than he could have imagined.

Sometimes wrong choices can be tragic—but you pick yourself up and try again. On January 28, 1986, the Space Shuttle *Challenger* exploded and broke apart after just seventy-three seconds into its flight, killing all seven crew members aboard. It was the first fatal accident involving an American spacecraft in flight. An investigation revealed the cause of the disaster was the failure of the primary and secondary redundant O-ring seals in a joint in the shuttle's right solid rocket booster (SRB). The boosters were essentially huge cylindrical tubes manufactured in sections, like sewer pipe, and joined together to make one object. The O-rings were part of the sealing system at each joint between two sections. These O-rings became weakened and failed under the extreme pressure and heat from the solid fuel.

In response to the disaster, the Space Shuttle program was suspended for thirty-two months while the Rogers Commission investigated and corrections were made. The next launch of a space shuttle was on September 29, 1988, and *Discovery* completed its mission. The program was continued until the second disaster—the loss of *Columbia* on January 16, 2003. The cause was damage to some of the space shuttle's heatproof tiles on the left wing, which failed under the heat of re-entry. The program was again suspended pending an investigation by the Columbia Accident Investigation Board (CAIB), and resumed with the successful launch of *Discovery* on July 26, 2005, and its landing two weeks later.

Failing is not necessarily a weakness, at least not in the case of Thomas Edison and his dogged search for the magic filament, but it can be a sign of organizational or personal inattention, or even malfeasance. In both of the space shuttle disasters, investigations revealed significant lapses in human judgment. In the case of *Challenger*, people at Morton Thiokol (the manufacturer of the O-rings) and NASA knew the O-rings were substandard but chose to ignore the warning signs. They ignored them because of budget issues and pure hubris; they thought the possible catastrophe would never happen. With *Columbia*, engineers discounted the significance of damage to the tiles from falling pieces of hard foam, were facing budget reductions, and were under pressure to maintain the launch schedule.

With these two tragic disasters, the engineers at NASA and its contractors learned a painful lesson: when lives are at stake, there can be no shortcuts.

Forgiveness

The space shuttle disasters raise the question of forgiveness.

Make no mistake—there was human error in both cases. In the *Challenger* explosion, you could argue that NASA and Morton Thiokol managers were negligent because they knew the O-rings were substandard and yet chose to roll the dice and hope they would not fail. But the unusually cold weather on the morning of the launch weakened the O-rings, and what the managers had feared *might* happen *did* happen. In the case of *Columbia,* it was more like inattention to a potential hazard. No one foresaw that chunks of falling foam could be a serious problem. Internal NASA deliberations had concluded it was an "accepted flight risk" and that it should not be treated as a flight safety issue.

Nonetheless, seven people died on each mission. We don't know how their families felt or how they responded; their grief must have been immeasurable. But collectively, as a nation, we chose to find the truth, fix the problem, and then forgive and move on. Unless you want to get mired in a dreary cycle of recrimination and payback, this is what you have to do.

Why failure and forgiveness to close out the book? Because everyone will experience failures and the critical aspect is, can you forgive yourself, learn from your mistakes and drive forward toward whatever goals you have created for your life. Having a clear sense of purpose and set of values that align your thinking and behavior with your vision and mission often enables you to forgive and move forward.

Our desire for this book was to inspire, motivate, educate, and support you in whatever your walk of life. Regardless of your vocation, career, or path in life, you can enhance your outcomes and the experiences along the way through the application of the methods discussed throughout this book. You can find through our website and social media pages and a variety of tools and ways to enhance your learning and journey. Visit us at www.becominginvaluable.com and commit to Becoming Invaluable personally, relationally, and occupationally!

Ready? Let's get started!

THANK YOU!

Thank you for reading this book. For more information or to just stay in touch, we'd love to hear from you!

We have many people to thank for helping us bring this book together. From those we have worked with over all the years and different situations, our interviewees: Jennifer Brotman, Dan Clark, Jim Gans, Dr. Ginger Decker, John Gronski, John Hardy, Jason Johnson, Tim Mitchell, Jim Voss, and countless others.

Our publishing group which includes all aspects of written, recorded and promotional activities associated with supporting the success of our book; "Becoming Invaluable"

Printed in the USA
CPSIA information can be obtained
at www.ICGtesting.com
LVHW051750071223
765728LV00056B/932